Easier, Simpler, Faster

Easier, Simpler, Faster

Systems Strategy for Lean IT

Jean Cunningham and Duane Jones

New York

Most Productivity Press books are available at quantity discounts when purchased in bulk. For more information contact our Customer Service Department (888-319-5852). Address all other inquiries to:

Productivity Press
444 Park Avenue South, 7th Floor
New York, NY 10016
United States of America
Telephone: 212-686-5900
Fax: 212-686-5411
E-mail: info@productivitypress.com

ProductivityPress.com

Library of Congress Cataloging-in-Publication Data

Cunningham, Jean E.
    Easier, simpler, faster : systems strategy for lean IT / Jean Cunningham and Duane Jones.
        p. cm.
    Includes bibliographical references and index.
    ISBN 978-1-56327-353-7 (alk. paper)
    1. Information technology—Management. 2. Business enterprises—Computer network resources. 3. Information resources management—Economic aspects. 4. Industrial efficiency. I. Jones, Duane, 1958- II. Title.
    HD30.2.C86 2007
    004.068—dc22
                                                                        2006102514

11   10   09   08   07   05   04   03   02   01

DEDICATION

To our friend, Joe Wilkinson, who made it possible for us to achieve
our goals of a system solution that worked with us, not against us,
and to our friend, Jeanne Belanger, for inspiring us to think
beyond our limits. May they both rest in peace.

For my husband, Alan, my father, Hubert,
and my sons, Schuyler and Chris
Jean Cunningham

For Daddy, who didn't tell me what I couldn't do.
Duane Jones

CONTENTS

ACKNOWLEDGMENTS

This book chronicles the application of one aspect of lean that was part of a pioneering course of change a small U.S. manufacturer led by a father and son team.

Pat Lancaster, Chairman of Lantech, recognized the winds of change in the late 80's and had the vision and courage to commit to lean in 1992 long before books on lean filled the shelves. Pat's prodigious leadership skills were exemplified in the way he provided continual high-impact advice and insight without "telling" us what to do or putting up roadblocks. He maintained a bubble of safety and permission that allowed all employees to bring their full enthusiasm and creativity to their daily work.

Jim Lancaster, CEO of Lantech, seamlessly took the reins of leadership in 1995 and to this day provides an environment of trust and change utilizing the power of lean business philosophy. Jim truly lives and works by the phrase, "Continuous Improvement with Respect for People."

Under Jim and Pat's leadership, lean is not "something we did" but "something we are." Those of us who were decisions makers and practitioners in Lantech's lean transformation are in Pat and Jim's debt and, frankly, we were lucky to be there.

Many thanks to Terry Brewer and Scott Wilkinson, leaders of TTW, Inc., for their commitment to lean in the development of their ERP product.

We would also like to express our thanks to Mr. Henry Kraebber, Jr., Professor of Manufacturing Technology, Purdue University, for his enthusiasm about lean and his dedication to introducing lean concepts and enterprise software to his engineering students.

We gratefully acknowledge Anand Sharma, CEO of TBM Consulting Group, for his encouragement and for supporting us in our quest to share what we have learned with others who are striving to make their organizations lean.

Sincere appreciation is extended to the publisher and editors of Productivity Press for their interest in this book and for assigning Gary Peurasaari as our editor. Gary's profound knowledge of lean has helped us clarify and bring to life our experience. His professional guidance made our task easier, simpler, and faster.

We are grateful to our spouses, Alan Riggs and Susan Jones, for their encouragement in this project and for their patience. We started talking about the book three years ago; all four of us look forward to seeing the work finished and the book in print!

Finally, it is our hope that by sharing what we have learned, we have set an example for our children. May they all find a life passion and the voice to express it.

INTRODUCTION

Lantech, Lean, and IS: Why This Book Was Written

Lantech, based in Louisville, Kentucky, has been in business for over 34 years and is a manufacturer of capital equipment, specifically packaging equipment. We develop and manufacture stretch, shrink, conveyors, palletizers, case erecting, and case packing equipment. Our vision is to be a global leader in secondary packaging equipment. Lantech does much of its work through internal product development, then manufactures and distributes through its sales channels. Though we are a small company (300 employees), Lantech has a variety of products that are sold and serviced by a network of 175 distributor locations. We manufacture high-demand products at a standard rate as well as very complex and unique products, all of which are custom engineered.

The authors of this book, Duane Jones and Jean Cunningham, have been associates and employees at Lantech for 17 years and 13 years, respectively, and were there during its full lean transformation in the job shop from 1992 through 1999, a process that included transforming Lantech's information system (IS).

Lantech began its lean business process in January of 1992. The thrust was aimed at improving all our business processes, using business process reengineering (BPR), a management tool that analyzes and then designs efficiencies in all aspects of a business workflow process, and running one kaizen event after another. A kaizen event is a brief team improvement activity for removing waste and implementing improvements in a work area. During the kaizen events, the Business Process Kaizen (BPK) team made a pledge not to make changes to the information system until it had made the processes themselves lean. That is, IS was about supporting improvements not driving them, so the BPK team wouldn't change IS unless it stopped them from making improvements. But IS became a barrier to the improvement efforts sooner than expected—when we were implementing cellular manufacturing and making improvements on our order entry systems, engineering processes, and accounting processes. The team's ability to continue its lean improvements slowed to a crawl because the information in the computer on the business side was completely inadequate to support lean. The data was simply irrelevant to what was occurring and needed on the shop floor. Some of the IS bottlenecks revolved around the seven deadly wastes (defined in Chapter 1). Specifically, the team uncovered the following forms of waste:

- Five different information systems located in different parts of the company
- Paying an outside vendor $15,000 a month, totaling $180,000 a year, to process information
- People throughout the organization reconciling data from one system to another
- People needing information about orders and not getting it
- Three different customer master files, two different part master and BOM files

Looking back on this, we wonder how Lantech lived with the dysfunction—it was mess. Our IS was totally out of sync and we had no way to run the business. Furthermore, we didn't have an IS transition plan to support manufacturing's lean efforts! As this book will show, however, the dysfunction was temporary. Though we lacked the skills, tools, and flexibility to do any major IS changes, our mission was to get the processes right before we started programming.

Thankfully, as our lean efforts eliminated waste and reduced the need for workers in these areas, we followed the lean principle of reassigning the most flexible and skilled people with the ability to lead other lean efforts. The discipline to relocate people is extremely tough—it takes time and effort to retrain—but the fact is these reassigned employees will become your new lean advocates. In our case, when we decided to find a vendor to implement enterprise resource planning (ERP), we called upon the reassigned employees that had worked with us in the BPR effort to choose the appropriate product to support our business needs. What we quickly learned was that even though these people were not part of the IS group and had no specific IS background, they were savvy about learning the IS and ERP language. Soon they became the core of our ERP implementation team, working with each business group to understand the data and process flow that IS would need to support. We did not adapt our business processes to IS. Instead, we adapted IS to our business processes.

Once we implemented the new ERP to run our information system, we needed to support it. Initially, we used tech/IT people for IT support, but these people, especially in a company of our size, are generally not interested in the continuous improvement cycle. As a result, we had high turnover—up to 100% in IS. When we took into consideration the wasted time spent training a programmer about our business *before* he or she could effectively work with the end user, we realized it might be more efficient to train people who already knew our business and culture, and understood the lean environment as programmers.

In their book, *Lean Thinking* (1996), James Womack and Daniel Jones highlight Lantech's lean efforts as a simple case study, stating, "Lantech is a striking example of what happens when a small American firm makes the value stream flow smoothly as pulled by the customer in pursuit of perfection." Because of Lantech's success with lean and transforming its IS operations to support it, approximately 80 or more people per quarter come to our manufacturing area to learn about what we have accomplished in manufacturing and lean business processes. There was, in fact, so much interest in Lantech's lean accounting, that Jean coauthored a book, *Real Numbers* (2003).

We decided to write *this* book to share Lantech's IS success story, to demonstrate what makes the IS change lean, why this is so important in a lean environment, and the changes we think companies need to make in particular areas to align IS to lean.

Beginning Your Journey: IS, IT, and ERP

Let's say that you are the information systems manager for your company and the CEO or manufacturing manager has just entered your office and informs you, "Manufacturing is going lean and we need you to help us in every way you can." What do you do next? You ask and answer two critical questions that can help you systematically and proactively begin the journey to lean:

1. What should your company do about information systems as it implements lean? That is, what changes will be required in the information system to make IS a partner with, rather than a barrier to, your company becoming a lean manufacturer and ultimately a lean enterprise?

2. What opportunities will arise for the information systems team to eliminate waste and apply lean principles in its own operations?

To find the answers to these questions, take stock of the *information systems* (IS) you have now and ask yourself if they have the capability for "converting, storing, protecting, disseminating, and retrieving" information in a way that fully supports a lean initiative. At Lantech, we use IS and IT (information technology) interchangeably. For this book, we will generally use IS for the broader discussion of information technology systems and use IT when dealing specifically with computer hardware and software. One such technology that the IS manager will need to review is the company's enterprise resource planning (ERP). Don't infer too much from the words creating the acronym ERP; somebody with too much time on their hands just strung them together and they stuck. What matters is what it does. An ERP system is an integrated computerized set of operations that, ideally, captures every facet of every operation a company performs. From a global perspective those operations would include Sales Order Entry, Engineering, Manufacturing, Inventory Management, Shop Floor Control, Purchasing, Accounting, and After-Market Service. Some people include Human Resources, and, lately, *front office systems*, like customer relationship management (CRM), which deals directly with customers. (ERPs are often called *back-office systems* because customers are not directly involved.) To support a lean initiative, a viable ERP system must have, at a minimum, the first set of operations listed above. Though there are ERP products that handle modules independently, the real strength of an ERP comes from having *all modules within central programming and central data,* that is, an accessible information system database that you can program and access. Having central data is enormously important for a lean company.

An ERP system can capture information in different facets of a company's operations, but traditionally this usually has not been a primary consideration for businesses when selecting and implementing an ERP. In a lean company, however, it is and should be a primary concern. In the daily course of performing the tasks that run your business, your ERP system captures and stores millions of pieces of information that become increasingly valuable for companies practicing lean manufacturing. To enhance and sustain its lean journey, a company needs to implement an information systems technology that works in tandem with and captures the necessary information for running a lean manufacturing operation.

All Value Streams Are Created Equal

Companies have many resources for understanding and applying lean techniques to their manufacturing processes, but lean principles also apply to nonproduction areas. When a company decides to goes lean, this decision affects all of its parts—all of its *value streams*. Value streams encompass all value added and non-value added activities and steps a company's products/services must flow through from concept, development, transformation of raw material, and delivery to and payment from a customer. The focus in lean thinking is continuously eliminating any type of waste in a company's *complete value stream*, waste that would otherwise drain resources away from creating value for the customer. In *Lean Thinking*, Womack and Jones discuss three broad management value streams that overlap and flow together:

1. *Problem-solving value stream*: Flows from the product design and engineering to product development and launch (administrative area).

2. *Information management value stream*: Flows from a customer's order to cash, including production scheduling and other nonproduction (office) activities for delivery (administrative area).

3. *Physical transformation value stream*: Flows from the transformation of raw materials to a finished product, to delivery to the customer (manufacturing area).[1]

A true lean enterprise is lean in all three of these value streams. Each process in an organization is a small part of these broader value

1. The value stream discussion was modified from *Lean Thinking* (1996) James Womack and Daniel Jones, *The Complete Lean Enterprise* (2004) Beau Keyte and Drew Locher, *Value Stream Management for the Lean Office* (2003) Don Tapping and Tom Shuker, and *Learning to See* (1998) Mike Rother and John Shook.

2. Value stream mapping is now a popular tool and there are several books on the subject, one of the first being *Learning to See* by Mike Rother and John Shook. During our lean transformation, we did not use the term *value stream* nor did we use value stream mapping. We worked to get our product families in as much flow as possible and then aligned our resources to that flow. We did not

streams, as its particular stream of output moves to the next downstream activity. One way to capture this is through *value stream mapping*, which visually maps the current state of the material and information flow of any specific process or set of processes (product/service family) and then helps an organization create a future state map to implement improvement processes.[2]

Over the past two decades, the activities and processes that typically occur in manufacturing (*physical transformation value stream*), have been the primary focus for companies going lean. Recently, several books have addressed the other two streams: *The Complete Lean Enterprise* (2005), for example, by Beau Keyte and Drew Locher, which focuses on the information management stream, and *The Toyota Product Development System* (2006), by James Morgan and Jeffrey Liker, which focuses on the problem-solving stream. Other books target specific areas and operations (e.g., lean for the supply chain, software, or accounting).

Unlike physical transformation and problem solving, an information system is not a typical value stream in itself, but it does *capture vital information for all three of the value streams*. For instance, all the customer order information goes into the ERP. This includes all the material requirements via a Bill of Materials, the costs of the organization, the information about which customers have ordered what products and services, their prices, and aftermarket issues. All of this information

---

organize all activities by product family, though we considered them in that light. Certainly, no functional organization was free from being pulled into the product family flow. Though we do not think there is necessarily an IS value stream, you can value stream map areas like Order Entry, the office, or other IS touch points to determine where you can eliminate waste. You can also align IS to help the lean process. In hindsight, we can now point to areas where you may be able to use value stream mapping, even though we have not used it in places where we have worked and consulted.

is not only critical to delivering a good or service, it also provides information that can be used to make decisions for the future. The point is that *your information system is one of the core elements that bind the entire company—capturing and leveraging information to enable and optimize all value streams.*

Overview

In writing this book, the authors elected to use a common sense approach, sharing stories and anecdotes about our experiences as we made changes, making it easier for the reader who is beginning the journey to capture the many lessons we learned along the way. Our lean shop, the ERP that supports it, and the authors' direct involvement with both transformations makes Lantech a strong model from which companies can learn. The Lantech model also provides an example of a lean conversion for IS technology in an already operating and successful lean manufacturing environment.

Chapter 1 covers a few lean principles, including the eight deadly wastes and thirteen IS guiding principles for implementing in a lean environment. In Chapter 2, we examine the role of standardization, an extremely important component of IS. Chapter 3 delves into the order entry process, and Chapter 4 discusses how Lantech selected and adapted an ERP that met the requirements of our lean needs. This brings us to Chapter 5 and the extremely important topic of kanban, a tool for procuring, managing, and assuring the flow and production of materials in pull just-in-time production systems. Kanban for your suppliers is an absolute necessity in a lean company, and this has huge implications for your information system. For the IS initiate, this will be an exciting topic because it completely changes the paradigm of inventory management and materials replenishment planning (MRP) or tracking part-related information. Chapter 6 discusses how to deal with MRP issues, especially in the tricky transition period between traditional batch manufacturing and cellular (pull) manufacturing. In Chapter 7, we revisit the ERP implementation stage and going "live" with the vendor on site. (This effort, by the way, garnered Lantech the Leonardo Award for Technical Innovations in Manufacturing, sponsored by Microsoft.) As noted above, the power of central programming and central data is enormous. For this reason, Chapter 8 focuses on our experiences using the capabilities of ERP for sharing information across the entire company and with suppliers and on using open information to build teams, trust, and a common lean culture. Finally, Chapter 9 will address some core changes you will need to make to your accounting practices and how to do this on the IS side. Specifically, we will show you how you can use the normal information system to do lean accounting without cost accounting. A short appendix provides the steps to use lean accounting on standard products.

To help tell our IS story, we have included computer screen shots and flow charts. We have also organized the material in a way that enables you to refer to various topics randomly, without having to read the book cover to cover.

Conclusion

Jean, acting as a lean consultant, once met with an IS director at a large company because all the early press seemed to imply that there was no need for a computer system to support lean. Everything was about visual management or control. The director wanted to talk with someone who understood lean but also understood the value of technology in a lean environment. We do not know if this is a widely held belief or not, but it is important to understand that it is *not* critical to have IT and ERP run the manufacturing portion of the processes, simply because a lean shop does not need complex production scheduling, Material Resource Planning for the materials requirements, or Standard Cost accounting. This is where ERPs traditionally have been very complex to run. On the other hand, the IS director was correct in thinking that you needed some technology. You will need to use the same ERP products that are readily available in the market and adapt them to meet the "new" information needs of a lean environment, specifically and especially for processing orders, billing customers, and closing the books. The ERP also creates new possibilities for collecting customer information that is vital to a lean organization. This book will help you to identify what changes you will make in IS and why, what is different about using ERP in a lean environment, and what remains the same.

Many people reading a business book find themselves thinking, "I do not do that. . . . I am not like them." But while it is true that no two companies are exactly alike, all companies have certain things in common and learning how another company has confronted and surmounted obstacles or designed and built a better system or process can be invaluable. Over the years, we at Lantech have accumulated a lot of knowledge that we currently share with various companies in many different businesses. So while your company, circumstances, and experiences are different from ours, you are likely to benefit from some of the decision-making processes and challenges we faced before and after implementing our information systems. What we learned along the way will help make your IS transformation effort more seamless. As we look back, we recognize that we didn't start in a straight line leading to a specific destination. But while we didn't always know where we would end up, we did use a lean approach—just doing it, learning from mistakes, correcting mistakes, and always asking, "Is there a better way?" We believe that *Easier, Simpler, Faster* will provide you with a broad vision as well as a path to the ideal lean system environment for your own company. We trust that this book will inspire you to take action as well as teach you to become a front-line lean-thinking leader. Enjoy the journey.

CHAPTER 1

Lean Basics to Define Your Customer Value, Eliminate Wastes, and Align IS

WHEN DEFINING THE LEAN ENTERPRISE in *Lean Thinking*, Womack and Jones were not only addressing manufacturing, but also marketing, distribution, accounting, and product development. Thus, as discussed in the introduction, your IS plays a vital role in delivering information to people who need it when they need it in each of these areas. Because many IS professionals are not well versed in lean thinking, this chapter presents a brief review of the mainstream lean principles.

The Five Lean Principles

Lean thinking is about using a systematic companywide approach to eliminate waste and add value for the customer. To accomplish these two goals, lean has five principles that work together: *value, value stream, flow, pull,* and *perfection.* According to Womack and Jones (1996), these principles are "the antidote to muda" or waste. The first principle is about defining your customer or value. The last four principles, which focus on building and delivering a product or service to the customer, emphasize eliminating waste. Below is a summary of the five principles.[1]

1. *Value defines the set of things that really matter to the customer.* The customer is the person who pays cash for a company's goods and services and ultimately defines the value of the product or service a company produces. More broadly, the customer defines each instance of value the company creates in its day-to-day activities to deliver a specific quality of product or service at a specific price and time. Value is about building the right product, and this means a company must know what its customer wants and needs. It must also understand its own business realities for meeting these needs. Ultimately, a company's value-add, and what it should produce, always comes back to how it defines its customer.

2. *Value Stream ensures that every business activity adds customer value (value to the product).* In the introduction, we defined the value stream as all value added and non-value added steps and activities that a company's products or services must sequentially flow through, including concept, development, transformation of raw material, and delivery to and payment from a customer. We then listed the three broad value streams: 1) *problem solving,* 2) *information management,* and 3) *physical transformation (manufacturing flow).* Companies must use continuous improvement to constantly identify and remove wastes in processes in each of these value streams to add value to their product or service.

---

1. References used to summarize the five principles and lean terms include *Lean Thinking,* by Womack and Jones; *The Toyota Way,* by Jeffrey Liker; *Lean Software Strategies,* by Peter Middleton and James Sutton; and other Productivity Press publications.

3. *Flow eliminates the non-value adding activities in the value stream so that a product's progression flows unimpeded continuously—from concept, raw material, finished goods, to delivery to the customer.* To achieve continuous flow, a company must develop and deliver a product with a smooth forward progress, ideally using *one-piece flow*. One-piece flow is arranging production (such as using *cellular manufacturing*) so that the products and services have a continuous flow through the various operations—design, order-taking, and production—one unit at a time, at a rate determined by the needs of the customer, or *takt time*, with the least amount of delay and waiting. To accomplish flow and strive for one-piece flow, you need a pull system and *just-in-time* (JIT).

4. *Pull uses a material replenishment system that is initiated by consumption—the upstream supplier doesn't produce anything unless the downstream customer signals a need.* The essence of pull is the production and management system JIT, a system of producing and delivering the right items at the right time in the right amounts. JIT pulls (withdraws) the needed item from the preceding process when it is needed to manufacture goods or services. The pull begins on the actual or expected customer orders, or *takt time*. The word *takt* refers to a musical meter, beat, or rhythm, or the baton of an orchestra leader. Takt time is the process of linking the pace of customer demand to the pace of production to the pace of actual final sales. The pull process continues by using *kanban* to pull needed parts from the previous process, which pulls from the process before it, and so on. (We will discuss takt time in Chapter 3 and kanban in Chapter 5 in more detail.)

5. *Perfection is the goal for eliminating all wastes along a value stream to achieve the idea of one-piece flow.* Once a company

works on the four previous principles and becomes "lean" it should be able to see its value streams clearly and continue to perfect them using *kaizen* (continuous improvement that strives for perfection and sustains lean on a daily basis) and *kaikaku* (radical improvement or kaizen blitz entailing a one to three month project). There are many other lean tools available to help achieve perfection.

As we unfold our lean story, you will see how Lantech applied some of these lean principles, exposing the waste and inefficiencies in our manufacturing, and how we adjusted our IS to support the lean process in our product families. In doing so, we developed thirteen IS guiding principles. Before discussing these, we need to review the seven deadly wastes, as well as make a few comments on kaizen, both of which play an important role in our IS story.

The Seven Deadly Wastes

To be an aggressive enabler of your business processes in all areas and value streams, your IS needs to adapt to your continuous improvement efforts to eliminate wastes. Waste is anything within a value stream that adds cost or time without adding value. If you do not work continuously to eliminate wastes, you cannot deliver on the five principles. Originally, Taiichi Ohno (the almost legendary designer of the Toyota Production System) identified the seven categories of waste around manufacturing as overproduction, waiting, transportation, processing, inventory, transport, and defects. We've added an eighth waste to this list: underused employee abilities or creativity (see Table 1-1). Lean practitioners have applied these categories of wastes to other areas of their businesses, such as product development, administrative work, and kanban for the supply chain. Though there are wastes in IS, focusing on these are not the emphasis of this book or your efforts. However,

Table 1-1. Eight Deadly Wastes

Definitions	Manufacturing/Material Wastes	Information Systems Wastes
1. Overproducing: Producing more, sooner, or faster than the next process needs; producing items for which there are no orders, or more higher-quality products than are necessary; increasing storage (inventory), transportation, damage, delays, and overstaffing costs.	Producing unnecessary materials, parts, components, or products before they are needed or manufacturing items for which there are no orders.	Overproducing information. Developing complex solutions to simple problems. Developing complex solutions to nonrepetitive problems.
2. Waiting: Time delays, process idle time, time on hand that impedes or stops work flow.	Waiting for people, materials, information, or decisions or waiting because of late delivery of raw material or work in process (WIP), lot processing delays, capacity bottlenecks, stockouts, and equipment downtime. Searching for schedules, tools, and materials.	Poorly developed reports or queries. Waiting for hard copy info instead of using electronic data.
3. Conveyance: Unnecessary transportation or multi-handling or temporarily storing and moving materials, people, information around, causing damage, missing items, or becoming an obstruction.	Moving material, work in process, parts, finished goods or information from place to place and/or into or out of storage between processes or over long distances causing delays.	Transferring data files between incompatible computer systems, software packages, databases.
4. Overprocessing or incorrect processing: Unnecessary, incorrect or redundant processing of a task, or processing higher-quality products than is necessary or processing with poor tools or improper product design.	Longer than necessary heat treatment, too many coats of paint, unnecessary or inefficient inspections, too many standards to adhere to. Excessive parts and/or direct labor tracking.	Overly reconciling because of different systems and having to enter the same information or orders in two or three systems. Overuse of technology when simplicity will do.

Table 1-1. Eight Deadly Wastes, *Continued*

Definitions	Manufacturing/Material Wastes	Information Systems Wastes
5. Excess Inventory: Producing, holding or purchasing unnecessary inventory, caused by wastes 1 and 4, which can take up space, impact safety, and become damaged or obsolete.	A build up of raw material, WIP, finished goods, or information required for a precisely controlled pull system, creating longer lead times.	Storing computers, computer parts. Outdated, obsolete information in databases. Too much data in transactional databases slowing down response time.
6. Unnecessary motion or movement: Excess activity, handling, unnecessary steps, poor layout (causing delay), or nonergonomic motion (causing possible injury).	Excessive walking during task execution, e.g., retrieving tools that can be used at the point of use, straining, looking, bending, or stacking. Wasting human activity on watching machines.	Keystrokes. Repetitive. Poor process design requiring combination of mouse and keyboard activity. Poor process design requiring reentry of data instead of reuse of data. Difficult to understand codes or titles for information.
7. Correction, defects, or processing failures: Rework, correction of errors, quality and equipment problems causing rework, replacement production, and scrap.	Failure to inspect and catch human and machine-made quality problems, having to fix an error already made, or fixing it repeatedly. Excess equipment failures and equipment downtime.	Out of date information. Unused reports. Hard copy instead of electronic copy. Fixing data late in the process stream versus collecting correctly in the beginning.
8. Underused employee abilities or creativity: Lost time, ideas, skills, and improvements by not empowering employees or tapping their creativity and talents to solve problems.	Decisions made by supervisors without input from hourly associates at the point where work is being performed.	Inadequate or unavailable computer hardware/software for employees. No channel to capture employee ideas or questions. Lack of schedule of when IS improvement resources will be available.

it is essential for your kaizen teams to understand these wastes at both the manufacturing and IS levels to identify bottlenecks and clear the way for an efficient information system.

Kaizen and Kaizen Events—Aligning IS to Improvement Activities

The Japanese word for "continuous incremental improvement" is *kaizen*. In a lean company, kaizen is the daily problem solving in more or less real time to address defects, errors, and abnormalities or improvements. Kaizen pushes the proposal and/or decision making for solving problems to the process owners—line workers and supervisors that actually do the work. The cornerstone of kaizen is the scientific method for identifying and solving problems, using such problem-solving methodologies as PDCA (Plan Do Check Act) or DMAIC for Six Sigma (Define Measure Analyze Implement Control.) At Lantech, we used "Ready, Fire, Aim" for our *kaizen events*:

- *Ready*: Identify the problem, brainstorm, and identify a solution.

- *Fire*: Implement the solution.

- *Aim*: Evaluate the impact of the solution to the problem and continue the cycle.

Kaizen events or kaizen workshops are improvement events. Typically a week long, they are conducted by a small team of people who identify wastes in the activities/flows of a process. Process mapping is one of the most important tools for directing a lean transformation, and the end result of a kaizen workshop is for the team to participate in implementing the new processes and techniques to achieve the improved future state. To ensure that these improvements are long lasting, kaizens also standardize these processes. It is during kaizen events that you put lean principles into action.

At Lantech, a kaizen event was a 3- or 4-day full-time work session involving 15 to 20 people from different processes and functions in the company, working together to solve a problem. The events were standardized with lean training, evaluating the current state or "as is" activities, brainstorming a completely new process using flow and pull, and then implementing as much change as possible. Every process and activity was fair game for a kaizen event. One important aspect of kaizen is that it teaches your employees various skills, such as solving problems in a group environment, documenting and improving processes, and collecting and analyzing data. Therefore, during each kaizen event, the team was fully empowered to make changes and all participants had equal voice and responsibility to participate.

Lantech conducted very few kaizen events specifically on IS. More commonly, as the product family-related processes had a kaizen, insights on how IS could support the improvements emerged and became follow-up items for the IS team. Usually, IS was actively involved with kaizen events, so the IS team members got a true in-depth knowledge directly from the events on how the processes in question would work. That way, the IS team did not need lengthy specs for systems adjustments or enhancements.

Thirteen IS Guiding Principles for a Lean Environment

During our journey, we developed thirteen IS guiding principles for a lean environment. Highlighted throughout this book, these principles are not hard and fast implementation rules, but rather an empirical compilation of lessons learned to guide you in your lean efforts. They will help you align your lean initiatives and remove waste in your IS system.

1. *Automate only if it is easier, faster, and complements your culture.* It is best to leave some things to manual efforts. You

don't want to install new technical systems for your processes just because they can do things faster. In our case, it was easier to do order entry manually rather than to create an automated transfer from a configured system. The effort required for the automation would not yield a corresponding return. In lean, it is better to assess technology carefully and adapt it only if it supports your culture and serves your people and processes.

2. *Build commonality to increase visibility and access to information.* Visual management or control is a key component of lean thinking. Providing easy access and standardized information empowers your employees and gives them access to the information they need to make decisions in real time.

3. *The primary purpose of security is to avoid data corruption and provide information access.* Information is what drives a business. Too often, security places limits on who can see what. A lean environment decentralizes its control system and includes the practice of open-book management, sharing financial information with employees. Decentralization means that everyone in the organization is empowered to audit, manage, and improve quality, cost, and delivery— locally and in real time. To do this, people need unimpeded access to current information. So think of your approach to security as keeping data secure from inadvertent change or corruption.

4. *Nothing lasts forever.* Either your business will change or software/hardware providers will develop new versions (or merge them). So think of your system decisions in terms of a five-year life span, and make your selection decisions on that basis. Adaptability is a key trait of a lean organization.

5. *Systems and software inflexibility can be the greatest inhibitor of change.* Lean companies are learning organizations, constantly improving and adapting to changes in the marketplace and to technology. If you cannot easily customize or adapt your systems and software for new processes or business practices and communicate them throughout the company, it will inhibit your company's nimble, lean efforts. It is best to adopt systems that have a demonstrated ability to adapt quickly and grow.

6. *Plain English system instructions are better than shorthand.* While power users love hot-keys and one-character inputs, they are very intimidating to new users and limit cross training and modifications to business processes. The best of both worlds are plain English data-attribute names, file names, and instructions, with one-character shorthand for the power user. Power users also want non-mouse inputs, while casual users or new users want point and click. Try to find both.

7. *Keystrokes matter to power users.* For users who do repetitive functions, like accounts payable or cash receipts, elimination of each keystroke removes waste and increases productivity. But use these quick shorthands only where high volume transactions are needed, because they can be very confusing to the infrequent user and impede training of new users.

8. *Capture everything you can about your customer.* This means using video, PDF, jpg, CAD, e-mail, you name it. Keep your options as broad as possible on the type of information to capture. Create an organized method for saving this nonstructured data about customers and orders. Knowing your customer is what defines your value as a company.

9. *Archive customer history; 'clean house' on internal transactions.* Not all data is created equal. Make choices on what to keep

long term. Inventory transactions have a short life. Customer orders have a long life—and are important for tracking trends. Even if it is cheap to purchase storage, housekeeping matters. It facilitates eliminating waste and helps keep your data organized and easily accessible for anyone.

10. *Capture information once and be done.* Capture quality information as early as possible in the process so others can use the information without having to recreate it. Take extra precautions, such as creating standardized processes, to ensure that the first time you capture information it is accurate.

11. *Use commonality to create an information highway.* Think of your information system as a highway with many entrances, exits, different speed limits, and as adaptable to trucks, cars, motorcycles—for the short-distance driver, as well as the long haul. Highways use common signage with easy, repeatable standard processes that make it easy to use the system no matter where you are located. It is necessary to have this standardized, multi-level and multi-usage capability for both your hardware and software so that users can access your information.

12. *Productivity for all is more important than productivity for one.* Few tools will optimize performance for every function, but you can organize your IS so that you align everyone across the organization to have easy access to the same data, assuring consistent quality information.

13. *Huge data stores are easy to manipulate.* Database and business intelligence tools make it easy to sift and sort through large volumes of information. Use the data you have collected to learn about your customer and business. The important thing is that your information system (and a module-rich ERP

specifically) captures every facet of your company's operations, a gold mine of data for any lean organization.

It is important that the reader keep in mind that IS efforts are about supporting the lean principles in a lean environment, especially in eliminating waste and adding customer value. Though managing your information system covers tasks that the customer does not see, it nonetheless adds value to producing goods or services. Chapter 2 examines standardized systems for IS, an invaluable way to make these tasks efficient.

CHAPTER 2

Applying Standardization to Information Systems

W HETHER THEY HAVE ONE CUSTOMER or one thousand customers, most companies have learned they have to give customers what they want. You have to customize your product to meet their needs and desires, be it a different color, an unusual size, different packaging, or highly engineered options. Regardless of what you provide, a common truth is that all companies need to modify their products or services to satisfy the customer. *Most of the time, they'd rather not.*

Evidence of this attitude is a question we have heard over the years, sometimes in frustration and sometimes in desperation: "Why can't the customer order what we want to sell?" Every company has a developed product that it believes will meet customer needs; most companies, in fact, have built a business model and profit plan around that product. It is no wonder then that we cringe a bit when customers expect us to deviate from our models and our plans.

Companies have different ways for managing the variety of changes required by their customers. They may stock a little of everything or overengineer a product so that it can easily be stepped down. At Lantech, we use the lean thinking way—build only what the customer buys. Regardless of how you deal with changing customer demands, you instinctively know that you could be more efficient and profitable if you could just manufacture and sell a standard product. To a certain degree, you are right.

There is an absolute value to having processes standardized, because it allows you to do the same activity the same way every time. The problem is that you probably can't push your standard product onto your customer (not for very long anyway). You can, however, take control and apply some valuable standards within your company to produce your products. The fact remains that standardizing is an absolute necessity for running a healthy company.

A well-known definition of insanity is doing the same thing the *same way* again and again and expecting a *different result*. True enough. However, doing the same thing in a *different way* every time and expecting the *same result* is equally an indicator of "imaginative" intelligence. Applied to processes, if you take the same task and do it differently each time, you will get different results. But, if you take the same task and perform it differently, your results may not only be different, they may be unpredictable. Running a business day to day presents you with enough challenges and complications without letting unidentified variables operate in any area of your business. Not when you have the ability to control them through standardization. The only way to establish this is by doing work the same way each time.

The point of having standards is to have the ability to detect the deviations of product defects, human errors, and abnormal process conditions and then correct them, ideally, in real time. To accomplish this you need operational standardization, for example, guidelines for quality, quantity, cost, inventory, and safety. However, standardization is also a visioning element of lean, representing the ideal way that the company knows how to do something at any given moment in time. This includes how you run your company, minimize waste, ensure the quality of your product, empower employees in processes, engage with all associates, and handle security. In lean thinking, establishing standards is your first step in creating a continuous improvement environment. In other words, without standardization you do not have the means to measure your work or improvement to determine if you are achieving the desired result.

Applying Standardization to Hardware and Software

Your information system is one of the prime areas in your company for applying standards and improving efficiency. Standardization is not just good for IS; it also enhances the lean philosophy of helping the end user. From a technology point of view, you need to determine how standardization works with the information in your company. Just look at some of the bad things that can happen if you don't include this concept in your IT policy for managing hardware and software.

The way Lantech ran its IS in the early 1990s provides a perfect example. Back then, we didn't have a centralized IS department or any policies regarding computer purchases. Each operational area had a computer nerd whose role was to determine the best computer and software purchases for a particular group. As a rule, these people didn't make bad decisions, but they never made the same decision twice. The purchases depended on what was on sale, what had a good write up, or what looked interesting that month. In addition, there was the occasional rogue buyer (usually a manager) who found a good deal somewhere and bought one or two PCs without consulting the computer nerds.

When Lantech finally got around to establishing a central information systems team, it faced a menagerie of PCs, different brands and makes and vintages, some Apple and some PC, with only a few departments' users using the same equipment and software. There are plenty of wastes associated with this type of ad hoc environment, but we didn't much notice because they were a low constant and stayed under the radar. It was when we saw the world through "lean eyes," that we discovered the hidden wastes that were there all along.

Hardware Madness

To illustrate the types of IT issues Lantech faced in the early 1990s, we'll look at three areas where our IS infrastructure was randomly structured. Many smaller companies will immediately recognize themselves, and many may have addressed some of these issues with new technology, going to LAN, and/or common software. The real question here is, "Have you gone far enough to remove all the hidden wastes?" Some of the most common are described below.

- *Spare parts.* How do you store available spare parts when you have twenty or thirty different types of PCs in your company? You probably don't since it doesn't make sense to keep a spare hard drive or motherboard or memory stick on hand when it is compatible with only two or three PCs. When a PC breaks, the best option is to send your computer expert to buy what seems reasonable at the time, adding one more variable to the mix. Of course the PC you scrapped will have some useable spare parts, so you can store it somewhere. When a similar PC breaks down months later, you can use those parts—if you remember where you stored the original PC.

- *Downtime.* What happens to the workers whose PCs are broken in the above scenario? If they are lucky (or have enough clout), they may have a new PC in a day or two. In the meantime, they will either do without or timeshare someone else's computer. If they have stored essential work on their own computer, then they are a little or a lot worse off, depending on whether the problem is a hard drive issue or if they saved their work elsewhere. Lantech never tried to quantify the cost of this sort of downtime because it is difficult to capture. Nevertheless, you know it's there.

- *Trickle-down effect.* Let's say that circumstances permit you to purchase a new replacement PC. What you are likely to see next is something we call "swap meet." Word comes down to Information Systems: "Take the new PC and put it on the desk of associate A and take associate A's PC and give it to associate B and then give associate's B's computer to associate C," the person whose PC died in the first place. On the surface, this makes sense because associates A and B are more busy, important, or efficient than associate C and will thereby benefit the most from the next generation computer. So associates A and B choose downtime while associate C gets a little more downtime waiting for the repaired computer to trickle down. Meanwhile, the IS associate spends time shuffling, reconfiguring, and transferring unique data among three computers instead of one. The truly inefficient part of this behavior is that associate C winds up with the oldest of the three PCs, and that PC is most likely to break down within the next year. Then the cycle begins all over again.

Software Galore

The issue that was probably the greatest nuisance at Lantech and in many other companies in the 1990s was the multiple word processor versions of Microsoft Word, WordPerfect, WordStar, and First Choice. In some ways, this nuisance was not as bad as you might think because back then, we printed everything out anyway. Nevertheless, it was a training and efficiency problem. When we were finally networked and employees could share documents, there was still the possibility that someone would save a document in an upgraded version of the software that someone else didn't have. Though each software package had utilities to open other document formats, you still could lose something in the translation. This is less of an issue in the 21st century because all the major software providers have developed global, world class standards. Moreover, if you go further and establish specific standardized toolsets, it is even less of an issue. Occasionally, however, bits of data are still lost or misread due to improper translation between tools and formats.

The subtler but more dangerous issue is not managing your software licensing. At Lantech, for example, we knew we had a lot of software installed, but we didn't know exactly where it all came from or who had purchased it. This also extended to the operating systems on the PCs. Another downside was that we hadn't bundled our software purchases, which would have allowed us to leverage the best licensing deal.

The different combinations of operating systems and applications meant that IS had to have pretty broad capabilities to troubleshoot all the potential problems, which is not an unreasonable expectation for techies but is nonetheless terribly inefficient. With so many systems, the possibility of seeing the same problem twice over a short period of time is slim, and this means you are always troubleshooting new issues or revisiting and relearning old ones instead of applying the same fixes to reccurring and known issues. This not only creates more downtime, it makes standardizing procedures or capturing lessons learned nearly impossible. Who has the time?

ERP in Name Only

We're using the term ERP loosely here. In 1995, Lantech had five different systems that employees used to run our business. Two of the tools were completely stand-alone and the other three were home-grown on the same platform, but were only able to share information after an external third party processed it. We had conflicting part numbers, customer IDs, account numbers, order numbers, and sales dollars, which meant we were wasting time in a constant state of reconciling. Often, the different systems would be used to process the same equipment order so the same information had to be entered in two or three systems. Then everything had to be reentered into the accounting package. Obviously, there was a lot of "overprocessing" waste just in transferring information, but there was also plenty of waste in arguing about whose information was the most accurate. Talk about failing to deliver value to the customer!

It should be clear by now that standardizing the hardware, software, and ERP can solve a lot of problems, but it is tough to change procedures when you are used to doing things a certain way. In addition, there are the financial and human resource concerns to consider. It is difficult to change systems that were based on somebody's wrong standard. But taking charge and making this change is a first major step for companies in this predicament. The many benefits will keep paying off.

Hardware Benefits from Standardization

Everyone at Lantech now has the same basic desktop computer using three possible configurations. The mechanical engineers have a high-end graphics card, the electrical and mechanical engineers have extra memory installed, and everybody else has the exact same "basic" configuration. For only a few hundred dollars, we can now easily store spare parts, keeping one or two of the primary components on one small shelf. If a PC goes bad, we can easily swap out whatever is required and get the user back to work. Because everyone uses the same basic PC, we can afford to keep spare ones in stock. If someone's PC goes out, we can get the user a spare one while we diagnose and repair the broken one. If it is the engineer's PC, we simply transfer the graphics card and memory to a new unit. With a common hardware and software platform, we reduce user downtime from days to minutes while managing spare parts and PCs (inventory) cost effectively.

We also replace or upgrade large segments of hardware at the same time. Now when we buy PCs in bulk from a single supplier, we know exactly the time frame and process warranty for all of our units. Buying PCs piecemeal made it nearly impossible to manage warranties.

Inventory, material replenishment, and cost savings improvements aside, one of the more important benefits of standardizing your hardware is that your IS associates will develop a deeper technical knowledge base and standardize known solutions, making them more efficient in distinguishing major problems from minor ones, solving them more quickly, and thereby improving employee efficiency and morale. Whether your company is small or large, reducing the computer options allows you to have an orderly replacement system, a manageable inventory for parts and/or PCs, and a knowledgeable tech staff to keep your workers adding value rather than falling victim to the waste of downtime, waiting for someone to "sharpen your work tools."

Software Benefits from Standardization

The gains on the software side were similar to those on the hardware side. We started by standardizing the operating system and word processing and spreadsheet tools for every desktop on Microsoft Windows 2000 and the MS 2000 Office Suite. We then migrated the bulk of our desktops and laptops to Windows XP and Office 2003. (Standardizing and staying with the Microsoft toolset allowed for a gradual version upgrade with no loss of functionality.) Everyone now has the same version of Microsoft Word and Excel and can share documents across the company. As a result, users are developing a common skill set, making it easier for associates to share work, back each other up, and transition to other positions, which means they spend time mastering a particular task rather than wasting time being trained. Sharing documents and using common skill sets has helped employees become more comfortable with storing and sharing documents electronically, rather than depending on hard copies. This, of course, is a major business advantage.

As with the hardware, standardizing software has made it easier for the IS team to recognize and solve problems. Reconfiguring PCs is also simpler. In addition, Lantech has an imaging application that takes a snapshot of all the software installed on a PC and then downloads that image onto another unit. The process takes about 15 minutes—a great improvement over the couple of hours it took to install Windows manually, particularly if something was missed during the initial download and the program had to be reinstalled.

Doing More with Less, Faster and Cheaper

One measure of how effective our standardizing effort has been is that we now have fewer, but more productive, employees on our IS team. Ten years ago our IS team had three associates dedicated to managing the network and PCs. Since then, the total number of associates has increased only about ten percent, but the number of people or tasks using PCs has increased by over fifty percent. During this same period, sales have increased over one hundred percent, and we have added several new servers and applications. There are never more than three people managing the network and PCs. Obviously, this would not be possible without standardizing.

How do you cost justify replacing every computer in your business at the same time? By recognizing that whether you like it or not, you are going to make a capital expenditure to replace them over the next three to four years anyway. You can pay cash up front with low interest rates, amortize the cost or lease the equipment, or use a bulk purchase with a bundled package to reduce the cost per unit, which is especially nice around quarter- or year-end. Regardless of how you pay, your budget needs to include the expense of purchasing IT, so there is no good reason not to do it at one time, especially with the gain in real productivity you will get by having everyone on the same hardware and software at the same time. As technology advances, your upgrade cycle will evolve. Our standard user desktops are now over five years old and high-end CAD stations are out to 24 to 36 months. The cost savings of taking waste out of the processes and having fewer IS people delivering a faster, more effective service, is justification enough.

More importantly, standardization of your computer hardware and software is a prerequisite to aligning IS to your lean environment. Implementing this improvement is part of IS guiding principle #2, *Build commonality to increase visibility and access to information*, and principle #11, *Use commonality to create an information highway*. Standardizing is a gigantic step in giving employees access to the same common tools to access the "same" information, with an information highway with common signage and repeatable processes. As you will see elsewhere, applying principles #2 and #11 helps your employees make decisions from accurate common information in real time, giving them more control in their decision making, which is a powerful lean concept.

Benefits from Using a Common ERP System

We mentioned earlier that employees using different systems and databases run the risk of disagreeing with each other on which data is the most accurate or correct. Employees cannot make a good decision when they are not certain whose new order entry is correct or sure about the cost of your inventory. Arguing will most likely fail to resolve the issue of irreconcilable figures or data. If employees have to drill back into the system and recheck or find "correct" data, they are practicing the "art of muda." Even worse, employees might make decisions independently, without considering coworkers' information, behavior that can be detrimental to the company.

A common ERP system means that everybody is viewing, discussing, and making decisions from the same standardized information. Sales dollars, inventory dollars, schedules, and purchases are always the same no matter who views them. Employees can still argue about what to look at (and they do), and they can still argue about what to do about it (and they will). But they can now confidently arrive at decisions that are supported by accurate and common data.

A common ERP system means you need fewer people to do the work, and you eliminate the waste of entering and reconciling information. When Duane joined the scheduling team in the Standard Products Division, there was a person in the division whose main responsibility was entering the sales orders from one system into another system and then making sure the data and subsequent invoices matched. With a common ERP system, we no longer transfer and reconcile information from one system to another. One person puts the information in one time, and it's done. There is no double handling, no duplication of effort. Nobody wastes time or money doing the same thing twice. This is practicing IS guiding principle #10, *capture information once and be done.*

Simply put, a standardized ERP system gives you a common toolset that makes it easier for employees to transition to another job or fill in for someone. All you need is a basic knowledge of how the tool behaves, and you go from there. When Lantech had five different systems, each group had to overstaff to cover for vacations and other absences because even though numerous other people in the company knew the process of the job, they probably didn't know how to use the ERP tools required in a particular area. This is no longer a problem.

It would be remiss not to mention one potential disadvantage to having a single overarching ERP system: it does not always give users the absolute best of state-of-the art tools for individual processes or departments. When we began looking for a solution to our systems proliferation problem, one consultant encouraged us to consider a "data warehouse" that would do just that. He would help us build a structure to hold all of our data and then we could purchase the "best of breed" application in each area to access the central "data warehouse." This sounded good on the surface because central data is a good thing, and buying the best tool for a specific job seemed to be an equally good thing. After all, when a tool is designed to specialize on one particular part of the business, that tool will outperform a "generalized" tool that is designed as a part of a complete ERP package. The problem with this entire premise is that there are application tools that specialize in accounting, marketing, leads, inventory, purchasing, and almost everything else. And while they have superior functionality to a similar integrated application tool and give every end user "the best of breed" to do a particular job, it may be more than what you need. The big question here is "Do they need it?" or does an overarching ERP provide more or less the same results?

If you consider IS guiding principle #5, *systems and software upgrades can be the greatest inhibitor of change,* you won't be deceived. You will immediately see that purchasing these "advanced" applications will invariably create a huge continuous task of always having to make sure the myriad applications correctly share information. You can do it, and there may be some benefits, but you will hamstring your IS people by forcing them to spend all their time managing your data and applications and upgrades rather than finding new ways to help the end users actually use the collected data. Once again, your employees will develop a discrete knowledge and skill set needed to run only their small unit of the business, making your resources less flexible and less lean.

Before describing Lantech's experience in choosing the right ERP package, we need to look at some important lean tasks we performed, namely, improving our order entry process. Traditional companies neglect this important "accounting function." For a lean company, tracking order entry and collecting its data points is an essential, ongoing task.

CHAPTER 3

Integrating Your Order Entry into the Information Highway

T WO OF THE MOST COMPLEX AND IMPORTANT AREAS of your IS in a lean environment are Order Entry and Order Management. Both are important because lean manufacturing does not require you to produce to forecast stocking levels or maximize the operation capacity of the facility. The premise behind lean manufacturing is that *you produce to the demand level of the end customer*, and there is no better way to know the demand of the customer than to shift the company's focus to new, incoming orders.

In lean companies, the demand rate of the customer is called takt, which was defined in Chapter 2. The German word for the baton held by an orchestra conductor, takt is the tool that shows the rhythm and rate for every orchestra member as they read the music and play. Likewise, in a factory, all functions need to have the capability to see and operate at the same rate as the pace of customer demand. The simple formula for determining the average takt time for the final process for any particular value stream is *takt time = net available operating time divided by total daily quantity required*. When the factory "plays" too fast, it creates overproducing wastes, such as overtime, overruns, obsolescence, too much inventory space, excess machine functionality, too much cash invested, and so on. When the factory plays too slowly, it cannot meet the rate of demand of the customer, creating waiting waste. Waiting for people, materials, information or decisions upstream (a bottleneck) may cause people in other areas of the factory to produce too much, resulting in excess expediting. With IS, waiting for approvals, or searching for information can also cause bottlenecks.

Every financial statement begins with the revenue of the goods and services that a company has shipped. The traditional way of looking at financial statements is to review financial statements to get an idea of how the company is performing. Although understanding what you have shipped is good, lean thinking requires that you *understand where your business is going.* Specifically, it means focusing on your Order Entry, new orders that have come through the door from real customers and on changes to existing orders, or the changing value of orders. This means asking questions at the right time (see Figure 3-1).

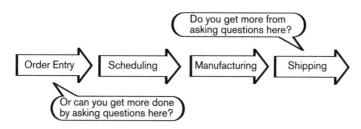

Figure 3-1. Focusing on Order Entry

Shifting a company's focus from shipped orders to new orders is important to the entire organization because the entire organization must work *to the pace of the customer demand.* The lean company is making just what the customer wants, in the configuration the customer wants. The customer drives daily performance. Returning to the lean principle of value, the customer defines each instance of value the company creates in its day-to-day activities to deliver a specific quality of product or service at a specific price and time. In traditional production, it is critical to manage complexity on the shop floor, which is not designed to accommodate one-piece flow production. In a lean shop, you do not have to worry about complexity. The lean shop already has the capability to design, order take, and produce one piece at a time as determined by the needs of the customer, or takt time. Every day, without delay or waiting, the lean shop responds to customer demand by saying "yes" to complex customer requests. This is why the key information for a lean company consists of new order rate, new order content, and new order value.

Modifying ERP to Handle Order Entry

Historically, few companies focused on the financial value of Order Entry. If they did, the focus occurred in a separate system and was not integrated into any type of financial module. When you create a debit and credit with an ERP system, an *accounting transaction* occurs immediately throughout the system, but it does not create an actual debit and credit when you enter your Order Entry. This is because Order Entry was not included in the traditional nonlean financial statement. In one of our Business Process Kaizen (BPK) team events, it did not take any deep analysis to determine that we needed to make Order Entry one of the first areas of business process improvement. We also determined that Order Entry must be included on the financial statement (at Lantech, it was placed on the first line). This was not an easy adjustment. Because most ERP systems do not track Order Entry dollars from a financial perspective, we had to make the changes manually while concurrently defining and developing the systems needed to automate the process.

Rather than creating separate reports each month for order entry, Lantech used the capability of the debit- and credit-generating ERP system to create debits and credits for order *entry transactions*. (Since an order does not change the profitability or balance sheet of a company, it is not a *financial transaction*.) We could easily do this because the

> ## Making Customer Order Changes in Real Time
>
> Making products to specific customer orders quickly leaves little room for adjustments to the customer purchase order, but the lean organization has a way of dealing with order changes when they do occur. Traditionally, from an information perspective, the impact of Change Orders on Order Entry numbers meant that if there was a change to the value of an order, the value of that order change was not included in the current month's order entry report. Instead, it was simply added to the original order, which meant any reporting would show that order with its value changed to the original date. However, using this practice means that historical data is always changing. If for example, at the end of last year you had $75 million worth of orders, changes to orders made in the current year would be entered as prior year data. As a result, your prior year information and performance would constantly change in value.
>
> To prevent this, the accounting and sales teams can enter the value of the change in order dollars in the month the changes actually occur—as normal monthly data or even in the daily report. This resolves all the problems with the changes in value of order entry and makes any reporting for commissions or bonus purposes easier. The role for IS is to support this change in a way that modifies traditional order reporting programs.

ERP functionality always creates a two-sided entry (a debit and a credit), so it was a simple matter of having ERP create a debit and credit to Order Entry account numbers. Not every ERP system on the market will have this flexibility, but flexibility is something you need. As stated in IS guiding principle #5, *Systems and software inflexibility can be the greatest inhibitor of change.*

With any ERP system you use, the same rationale applies. You ignore and never report one side of the transaction because it does not actually affect profitability. You simply credit an account for any new orders in a given period and ERP immediately registers the order entry information. Because it is just like any other data associated with a transaction, you can cut it in all ways, such as by product line or by region. As part of the normal reporting, you can review the order entries for product A, B, or C daily or as needed (and as part of the monthly reporting package), and directly feed current customer demand for each product to the lean shop. Using the capability of ERP to focus on order entry is a critical and necessary change a company needs to make to its information system if it is to enable its lean manufacturing. Using ERP to focus on order entry is a change from how most companies use ERP products and is essential in supporting your lean enterprise.

Every Employee Sees the Customer Order

When operating a lean company, the most important information is not necessarily on a financial statement (although at Lantech, every income statement at the product line level and at the summary level has Order Entry at the top of the page). What is important is to highlight the order information in other places. For instance, use the banner in the ERP system to place messages of the day that everyone sees when entering the system. Lantech uses this banner to show the order entry and shipment levels. Every person, regardless of his or her job, immediately sees the order entry level, month to date. This communicates the strong message that the most important things are customer orders and reinforces the lean principle of value—know your customers and focus on them. Furthermore, no one has to wait for corporate to say how you are doing. Every person in the company already sees how you are doing from the volume of orders received and performs his or her work accordingly. While Lantech holds monthly company meetings to inform and interpret the company's progress and numbers, people already know the most important information on a daily basis throughout the month—the level of orders.

Visually displaying this information decentralizes information and empowers every individual to take personal ownership and responsibility for the business on a daily basis, as work is being performed. This ensures that orders are being filled and that employees are eliminating, on the spot, any obstacles to that goal. Decentralization of decision making so your employees can access information in real time to make real decisions is essential for operating a lean environment and an important component of IS guiding principle #2, *Build commonality to increase visibility and access to information.*

Handling Incomplete Customer Orders

Lantech's relentless focus on order entry, however, did cause a new problem, something we call the *pre-order entry-holding pen.* Lantech wanted to see its customer orders as soon as they came in from the field, which meant getting those orders off the street immediately and bringing them in-house. The sooner the orders were in-house, the sooner they belonged to us and not the competition. This was a very important strategy for us, but it created more of the seventh deadly waste (correction, defects, or failures) by creating redundancy and rework in our business processes because initial orders were often entered with incomplete or incorrect information (see Figure 3-2).

When an order comes in with incomplete and confusing information, there is an immediate conflict: Should we enter the order in the system or not? We don't want orders with incomplete information in the system, even if they are lucrative orders for important (and expensive) equipment. We particularly don't want orders in the system that are missing any key information that manufacturing needs to have. This is especially true for lean manufacturing, which builds to customer orders using takt time, thus making both lead time and the opportunity to adjust an order short. At Lantech, it is less than one day for some products. Depending on the amount of work that is going

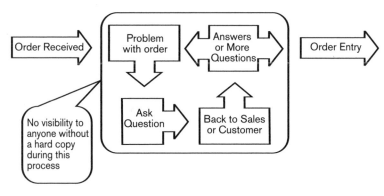

Figure 3-2. Flow Before the Pre-Order Entry Pen Process

into "building to customer orders," the available time could end up being very short. If we go ahead and build a machine with, say, incomplete ship-to location, major wastes are created in terms of providing available floor space to hold the machine, taking time to exchange telephone calls or e-mails to update information, and, of course, updating the order.

Lantech's BPK team decided not to release orders with incomplete information live into the ERP system. But this decision subsequently barred us from using some of the ERP features to communicate electronically with customers, distributors, or internally with engineering or other departments that might need the information or that might provide answers to issues related to such orders. These features include e-mail, standard template letters, alert systems, and the like, and not using them was counterproductive. The BPK team decided to put orders with incomplete information into the system with an electronically designated "pre-order" status, meaning that we now had an incomplete but valid order. They achieved this by programming the system to upload an incomplete order without creating a debit and credit or showing financial information. Instead, the orders were now available for use in an e-mail alert system to notify people that we needed information or that the order was incomplete. The rest of the company could also see the outstanding pre-order entries; by clicking on an order, people had access to its entire history: Who needed to do what to finalize, manufacture, and ship the order to the customer (see Figure 3-3).

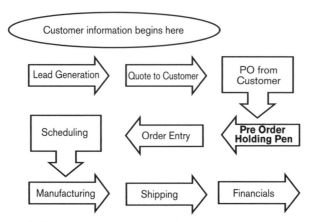

The flow is one step at a time, one after the other with no retracing or jumping forward out of step. Employees have electronic visibility for all information about each step.

Figure 3-3. Flow After Implementing the Pre-Order Entry Pen Process

The pre-order entry-holding pen eliminates much of the rework and redundancy. Besides "pulling" information from those who need to provide information to complete the order, it also contains status information, such as the date an order comes into the system and how long it has been there (see Figure 3-4). The pre-order entry-holding pen tool has been very helpful for the company to get the order off the street, communicate information about an order to those who need to see it, and then manage the order (using the ERP tools) by making it clean and ready to manufacture. Engineering and manufacturing no longer work on incomplete orders because they no longer receive incomplete or inaccurate orders.

The whole focus in lean is to eliminate waste and create a pull system based on customer order demand signaling a need to produce. In

Ident	Ship to	Date received	Stat	SM	Type	MD	Prjmgr	PO #
00000605	KENSENG PRINTING CO	Jul 07 2006	ADF	KWF		QX		05807469
00000567	L & K CONCRETE AND BLOCK	Jun 28 2006	TECH	IAS	STD	QA	CAROLEL	22108
00000607	MIDWEST BOTTLING CORP	Jul 07 2006		CJK	STD	CV	SHERRYW	33605110
00000606	ABC AUTOMOTIVE	Jul 07 2006		MJC		QM		82272
00000604	HENRY GROCERY DISTRIBUTION	Jul 06 2006	ADF	KWF	STD	CS	SHERRYW	8S37920D
SW00198-00	CAUSEWAY FROZEN FOODS	Jun 08 2006	OTH	KWF	STD	SW	CAROLEL	8S82469D
SC11484-01	DONG-NING LTD	Jul 07 2006		ENB	CPX	SC	RONC	GM813299MS

Figure 3-4. Pre-Order Entry Holding Pen Status Information

a pull system, using cells, kanban, standardization, or standard work is also essential for just-in-time delivery (JIT). As you can see, order entry is not merely a financial issue; it is the tool or information that signals what your customer wants and when they want it, which starts the whole just-in-time system rolling. One of the first things the lean system leader will want to do is develop the pre-order holding pen and align the information system to focus on product line new orders. Once you do this, your takt rate will be more accurate, and you will then be able to integrate your order entry into both your financial and reporting tools. This will empower your employees to load and retrieve consistent and accurate information in the month something occurred, as well as to see how order volumes change over time (see Figure 3-5).

IS guiding principle #12, *Productivity for all is more important than productivity for one*, is about using tools to align everyone across the organization, and this means using tools to organize your information system so everyone in the process has access to the same data when they need it. Although implementing the pre-order holding pen is an additional data entry process that someone will need to perform, this is a minor inconvenience and is offset by the advantages of increased visibility: seeing at a glance what your customers want and when they want it.

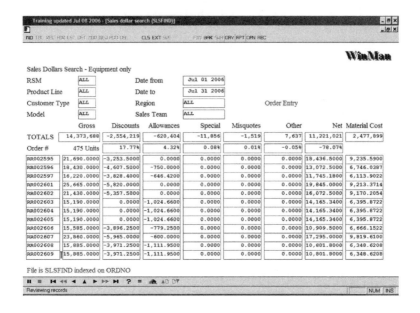

Figure 3-5. Pre-Order Entry Holding Pen—Sales Dollars

Make Your Office Lean—Less Paper/Immediate Access

Order writing or the internal order support process is one of the more wasteful processes in information systems and cuts across nearly all the wastes, yet most companies, even lean ones, have not standardized the work flow for the traditional "office job." Over the years, companies have usually relied on clerical personnel to develop the detailed paper flow for getting work done. Most often, these processes were haphazardly designed around a batch and queue approach without much regard to the organization as a whole, and most specifically to takt time processes.[1] This is a great opportunity for a company to use the IS team

---

1. Though we did not use value stream mapping to identify waste and to implement lean in our administrative (office) area at Lantech, there are several books in the market explaining this. Among the best are *The Complete Lean Enterprise* by Beau Keyte and Drew Locher, and *Value Stream Management for the Lean Office* by Don Tapping and Tom Shuker.

to help harness the experience of its office support to create a lean process. The following story from Lantech's history shows how valuable the IS team can be.

In what was once a typical process at Lantech, an order would arrive, usually via fax. The first job was to create a file folder with the name and order number on the tab. This was, believe it or not, done with a typewriter, which many organizations continue to use even in the 21st century. An office worker then entered the order into the order entry system and into the manufacturing system. He or she would then make copies of the order, the purchase order, and the Application Data Form (ADF), and enter these in the file. (The Application Data Form was valuable in a job shop business because each order had to meet a unique customer application. Moreover, the application fit was so difficult to capture we would ask the customer to describe exactly how they were going to use the equipment. In connection with this, we asked for the type of product to be packaged, the speed, the adjoining equipment, and the type of environment—indoor, outdoor, cold, hot, etc. This was the only way to ensure customers got what they really needed.)

The office worker would make an additional copy of this packet of customer information and deliver it to the people who had responsibility for the order. This included the salesperson, the engineer, purchasing, the scheduling office, and the after-market service. Each person/department needed this information to plan for supporting and completing each order. Only then would the actual work on the order begin. Simple and familiar, right?

Hold That Order!

At this time in the company's history, every order had the potential of revealing some new problem. An engineer found an inconsistency between the customer order and the customer's Application Data Form; field service did not have a qualified technician for the planned date and equipment type; purchasing could not get the special conveyor to

---

When the Order Entry Process Becomes
an Obstacle to Lean

How do you know when you need to overhaul your order entry process? A good indication is when the lead time for entering an order takes longer than the lead time to produce it—a serious misalignment with your takt time. Implementing kanban and cellular production at Lantech made such an impact that within one year we had a one-piece flow manufacturing process that was faster than our order entry process. Meanwhile, the order entry process was burdened with waste: entering information into two systems, multiple checking, and approving. That was in addition to waste created by the physical file. Each step was full of "waiting" queues, causing a bottleneck for the work flowing downstream to the job shop. It could take up to two weeks to process just one order! (The lead time for the products was from 4 to 20 weeks prior to lean and 1 to 4 weeks after lean.) To make matters worse, the delays sometimes caused later processes to play catch-up and expedite orders, which created quality issues.

---

the specification; or no one did a credit check on a new customer. Although some of these problems were internal, others arose when customers changed order requirements.

As each change issue was resolved, the office would update the order information, which meant someone had to make copies for six different physical paper-order files. Furthermore, the office would need to reorganize the new copies to replace the old information so no one inadvertently used it. Considering the opportunities for errors and outdated information, people still did a tremendous job, but it took a huge amount of time to keep everyone informed of every change.

The IS team needed a lean solution, one that eliminated redundancy, quality issues, and waiting time for entering, sharing, and retrieving information across the company. They also needed a quick solution that didn't require much money or training time. Because order entry was a serious bottleneck, the team looked there first and found a solution that met all of the criteria: Microsoft Windows Explorer. The BPK team converted any type of document for an order to a digital document, be it a purchase order, ADF, original quote, adjusted purchase order, adjusted ADF, shipping agreement, confirmation document, invoice terms, and so on. All the documents were then identically and immediately available to every person using the order information. Electronic sticky notes were used to post comments on documents as needed, making changes or new information visible for all to see.

There were definite tradeoffs using this solution. First, the document saved in "scanned" format was not individual data points that could be manipulated in a database, so it was not very useful to marketing. Moreover, the team had to establish naming conventions for the documents so that everyone could find the right documents.

The IS team investigated a couple of sophisticated document management tools that had considerable functionality and security beyond our simple Windows interface (and were more expensive), but Windows, which we already had, was sufficiently configurable and could be easily programmed to make it difficult to lose any information accidentally. Although someone could sabotage the data or delete documents, this was unlikely to happen. Because Lantech is not a bank or a branch of the government, we never felt the need for high-end, expensive solutions to secure data.

Regardless of your solution, the goal is to give everyone in your company direct access to identical, updated information. This is where IS guiding principle #3, *Primary purpose of security is to avoid data corruption and provide information access* applies; you don't want your security concerns to place limits on what employees can see. In addition, by using shortcuts to get the capability in place quickly, and tools that most users in the company already know how to use, you follow

IS principle #5, *Systems and software inflexibility can be the greatest inhibitor of change.* In your lean effort, it is best to adopt (and adapt) a system that the entire company can easily use; it does not have to be the best or most powerful system on the market.

From Lead to Quote to Order

As you move through the information system, the information highway keeps getting longer and longer with greater possibilities for bottlenecks. Lantech's BPK team began with the most obvious bottleneck, order entry, and integrated it into the information highway. Then it turned to quotes and leads, adding them in such a way that we could minimize duplicate entry of information. The best improvement and the one with the most impact was how we entered quote information and converted it to an order. As explained above, companies in the job shop business often have many customers with specific needs for a piece of equipment. Most of our customers have an established working relationship with the company and very few order something out of the blue (although those types of orders travel our "highway" too). This is how we now convert quote information into an order:

- Our customers tell us about their needs.

- We give them a quote that suggests the type of equipment they will need, and maybe some optional features as well.

- The customers consider the quote and some of them put their trust in us and give us a purchase order. Much of the same information needed to record the order is already collected in the quote process because our quote information-collection process and our orders have a similar format.

- When we accept a quote later on, we merely have to convert much of the information from quote status to order status since it is already in the system, thus eliminating redundancy and tremendously reducing the potential for errors.

Scheduling an Order to the Floor

In cellular manufacturing, the scheduling of the orders to the job shop floor is very simple—the next order received gets the next manufacturing slot. It is almost like lining up at the ATM. First come, first served. Well, maybe not quite that easy. Sometimes customers don't want immediate delivery or they need a machine on a specific date. In such cases, you put that order in a slot in the manufacturing schedule that will allow the shipment on the desired date, but at a specific takt time or production rate, which defines a certain number of slots to start and complete machines. When the office enters an order, a message automatically goes to the scheduler (who actually sits in the manufacturing cell on the shop floor), and he or she places the order on a *Big White Board* on the line. That Big White Board tells everyone on the line what is next and how many orders are on the line. If there is too much backlog, it may be necessary to change takt time; if there is too little backlog, there may be some open time to do improvements. Everyone on the line likes the Big White Board, but other employees like the setup, too, and may need the same information. Since the Big White Board was so easy for everyone to use and understand, we made a computer screen that looks like the Big White Board (see Figure 3-6). One side is for unscheduled orders and the other side for orders by day compared with the slots available. At a glance, it is easy for all employees to see the next slot open and the extent of backlog.

The information on the left has the number of scheduled machines by day and shows if there are any open slots. A detail schedule for the day also exists with the same detail as on the Big White Board. On the right, are any orders that are not yet scheduled and some indication of their status. This determines the "work" of the scheduler who assigns each order.

Most ERP systems have highly complicated extensive planning and scheduling modules working with routings, operations, jobs, and subjobs. Whether your company is reviewing your existing ERP or

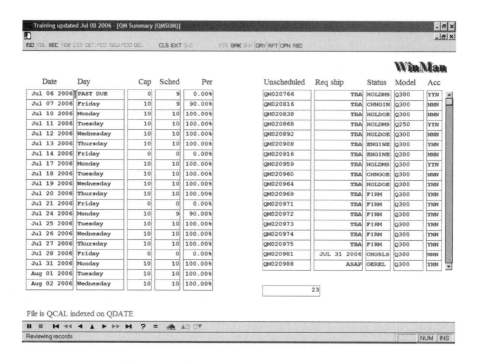

Figure 3-6. Big White Board Computer Screen

looking for a new one, you are probably paying or will be paying for this planning and scheduling module, which is a core feature of most ERP tools and seldom excluded. If you are dealing with a slick ERP salesperson, he or she will work hard to make you believe you can't do without it. You can. *We don't use it.*

Implementing and maintaining a normal planning and scheduling tool requires a huge investment of capital and human resources. The good news is that for companies in a lean manufacturing mode, such tools are a waste of time. To make your IS lean, you need to drive your new process enhancements around new orders and order entry. The payoff to improving lead time is huge, but so is your customer's perception of you. Your front-end order processes are the most visible processes to a customer—you are constantly focused on them and they know it—and this can immediately create real competitive advantage.

Ultimately, a company's value add always comes back to how it defines its customer, and your front-end process contributes to understanding and delivering what the customer wants.

The next chapter brings us to the process of choosing, reviewing, and implementing an ERP system that supports lean. There are several steps and issues to consider, such as customizing, that will help you find the right ERP solution for your particular company.

CHAPTER 4

Selecting, Enabling, and Customizing Your ERP System

L ANTECH BEGAN THE SEARCH FOR AN ERP SYSTEM in late 1994. In May 1995, the new ERP team had chosen WinMan, and implementation began in early July. We went live on October 1, 1995 (covered in Chapter 7). Some aspects of this selection and implementation were contrary to standard practice: Some of our choices and operating philosophies evolved from the process rather than from the policies dictating the plan. This approach worked. By the end of 1995, we were satisfied that the project was a success; the choices and decisions we made continue to show a healthy return on our investment. This chapter will cover a few essential elements that guided our search for a new system. We believe these elements will be useful for others who are embarking on a similar journey: success in selecting and enabling the best ERP solution.

Base Product Definition—Technology and Business Preferences

To make our core decision, we needed to be clear about our base product definition. Thus, the business process kaizen team (BPK) that had been using business process reengineering to improve all our business processes since January of 1994, identified the technology and business preferences criteria to define the type of ERP product that was best suited for Lantech. The technology criteria were absolute:

- The tool had to have a GUI interface
- It had to be Microsoft compatible
- It had to have a relational database (method of storing information that minimizes storage capacity and maximizes the retrieval of information)

The business preferences criteria were somewhat less stringent:
- The tool had to capture and integrate most but not all of our business processes
- The tool did not have to include payroll or human resources

Looking back, we realize we didn't fully understand some of the deeper technology decisions that we made and our choices may appear simplistic or obvious to some readers today. Regardless, before the new ERP team began its detailed process of selecting a system, it had established clear standards that enabled them to narrow their scope and eliminate months of research and discussion on every possible system.

Use Business People with Lean Backgrounds to Find a New ERP System

The next step was to create a new ERP team, which, at first, consisted of one person. Our first team member was Jeanne Belanger, who had been serving as one of Lantech's purchasing and manufacturing managers. Jeanne spent several months working alone culling through 300 products to identify ERPs that were compatible with the technology and business preference criteria chosen by the BPK team. With clear standards for selecting the system in place, Jeanne was able to narrow the scope of the search, thus avoiding months of research and useless discussion about the advantages and disadvantages of every ERP system in the marketplace. She later drove vendor interviews.

The new ERP team was eventually expanded to include the five core members of the BPK team, each with a business background. One of these individuals was Duane Jones, whose background was in manufacturing with experience in purchasing, engineering, and sales. By the time Duane joined the new ERP team, the ERP candidate list was small enough that each potential product could be thoroughly reviewed.

The reader, at this point, may be wondering why the IS team was not included in this process, and this is a valid question. At the time, Lantech's IS team was quite small and IS team members were fully occupied with maintaining existing systems that could not be neglected during the search process. The IS team, however, did play an important role in the process and the contributions of the team are outlined below.

BPK team members Mike Balough and Jean Cunningham became the project sponsors for the new ERP team. Jean doubled as a project coach, while Mike functioned as liaison with the IS team, which focused on getting the building ready for a common network and linking up all the PCs. This was a prodigious job, especially because IS was already engaged in keeping the existing systems running smoothly.

The fifth member of the team was Rick Norris, who had been Lantech's scheduling manager prior to lean implementation. His role on the new ERP team was dealing with the sales and sales support areas.

One of the things that facilitated the entire process was that the new ERP team consisted of five people who really understood all the lean processes that Lantech had implemented during the prior two years. In addition, most of the team members had firsthand experience of lean restructuring. With the exception of Jean and Mike, the jobs they held prior to lean implementation had been eliminated. The best and brightest, they were assigned to the Business Process Kaizen team when their own positions were eliminated through their own lean efforts.

The important message here is that even if you have the IS capacity, it is not necessary to engage the IS team at this juncture of transforming your IS system. What is essential is to have a systems team with some business background, experience in lean, and the ability and willingness to dedicate themselves full time to the effort.

Beware the Techies and Bean Counters

The authors are not technologists (techies) and only Jean can claim experience as a bean counter. We moved into the IS ranks from the business side. You might find that unusual in information systems, but one of the things that we learned from implementing information systems is that it is extremely important to integrate them fully into the strategic decisions of the company. Traditionally, technologists are not in a position, nor are they trained, to do this. More importantly, a lean business would never hand such a task to a technologist who never walked a shop floor and/or did not know how to procure material. A technologist is not trained to recognize or discriminate between components that are necessary or peripheral in implementing a nonwasteful and company-appropriate information system. Not knowing what is best for the business, techies may merely be driven to purchase the latest technology, a cool toy to play with. Cool toys, however, do not make a company lean. Neither does purchasing the newest and best tool on the market. In lean thinking, you want the technology that you need, when you need it, with the capabilities that solve actual problems. More importantly, you use technology to help people to solve possible problems; you do not rely on technology alone to do so. The business and shop floor know what they need—they are the internal IS customer. For this reason, it is best to assign and align the people that really run the business to embrace, own, and integrate IS into your corporate strategy.

Skip the ERP Product Sales Talk and Go Directly to the Technicians

Early in the process, the ERP search team, visiting prospective companies Jeanne had selected, realized that time spent talking with sales people was usually time wasted. Almost invariably, the team asked the sales people technical and business process questions that they couldn't answer satisfactorily. We soon learned that the logical solution to this problem was to speak to the technician(s) behind the product. Once we had the right people to talk to, team members would visit them in their offices and invite them (along with the sales people) to Lantech.

Team members spent hours (sometimes days) crosschecking and testing product functionality and the underlying technology, and this was a source of great interest for some of the sales people and technicians who visited Lantech. Their interest sometimes took an amusing turn. The ERP search team used a large workroom for the project, and the walls of the room were lined with notes about the strengths and weakness of all the ERPs we had reviewed. Curious as to how they might measure up, or what we were up to, the visitors covertly scanned the walls, anxious to get a closer look but generally too polite to ask for permission to do so. Their longing gazes eventually caused occasional gaps in conversation, and we responded to this by giving them an opportunity to browse, ask questions, and learn what they could. This was not simply a matter of courtesy; during the process, the techies and salespeople came to understand our needs as well as our philosophy of openness in communication and information sharing, which was essential for our ERP program.

The Role of End User Participation

One waste that many companies may not even be aware of is number eight in the Table 1-1: underused employee abilities or creativity. By empowering our employees (those who actually do the work) to participate in the selection process we unleashed their ideas, skills, and creativity. From the beginning of the selection process, the ERP search team focused on having the actual system users define and ultimately find the right tool.

Three of the core team members had operations backgrounds. None of us had any significant project management experience for selecting and measuring the various ERP systems, so we invented our own. Our first priority was to create a checklist of the primary business transactions our company needed to perform as well as a list of things the ERP system had to do. The list came to about three pages and became the basis of our search criteria. Figure 4-1 shows some of the essential points. There are now numerous toolsets and consultants available on the Internet that provide a more exhaustive checklist than our three-pager. The fact that our three-page document did not miss

---

Information Systems Requirements

Platform:

Client Server:

Database Type:

GUI:

Bar Coding:

User Base:

Hardware Support:
    Off-lines
    Archiving
    Database management

Software Support:

Hotline:

Vendor Experience:

Figure 4-1. Essential Things the ERP System Must Have

any core functions is evidence that most companies have employees that know their business well enough to draft their own checklist.

The team also established a few basic questions about each ERP system's underlying technology and its compatibility with other common toolsets that were important to Lantech. As vendors demonstrated the specialty of their respective tools, we used simple metrics to evaluate them:

- How does this tool perform our business processes?

- Can we see the tool work?

- Does this meet the needs of what the end user needs to do?

After the team reviewed, researched and visited the home offices of about ten product vendors, we pared our list of candidates to a final three. Still focusing on user involvement, we invited each of the three finalists to Lantech to spend two days giving six two-hour reviews to the people who would be using the tool every day. We provided each vendor with a fixed script of points to cover and allowed time for general questions and answers. Between fifteen and twenty people attended each session. With six sessions, that meant around 100 people; thus, almost half of the company had a chance to evaluate each product. We collected feedback from the users via a questionnaire that included a general comment section. There were five important reasons for having the users deeply involved from beginning to end. The users:

1. validated the impressions of the search team regarding the strengths and weaknesses of each product;

2. highlighted issues that we would need to address with each product;

3. had some idea about the alternatives whenever they had frustrations with the final choice;

4. developed a consensus of the best tool;

5. knew they were a part of the selection process and had a vested interest in making the final choice work.

The team's attention to user involvement was one of the prime factors that helped us to identify and successfully implement an ERP. However, it is equally important to mention some of the things we *did not* focus on:

- *Executive reporting.* We did not look for a tool that was user friendly to managers, because they would not be using it. Instead, we looked for a tool that would perform our business process. If the tool could not run the business, then the reports would not matter. Although we did not entirely ignore executive reports, we knew that the ERP would be capturing management data and we could pull it out as needed.

- *Background technology.* We had a professional IT consultant, Roger Koebel of Kaizen Technologies, who traveled with us on occasion to advise us along the way. Roger was an excellent teacher and an invaluable resource, but in the few months he worked with us, he was not able to convince us that an industry standard database and programming language were critical to our selection.

Finalizing Our ERP Choice

After about a seven-month search, the team finally chose WinMan from TTW. WinMan runs on a Superbase engine, which, after thirteen years and millions of transactions, continues to work at considerably less cost than the more popular Microsoft SQL Server or Oracle. Both the database and programming language are easier to use with the Microsoft standards.

In the beginning, we had a couple of concerns. TTW is a small organization, and we wondered what we would do if the company were unable to develop the tool to our specifications or went out of business. In addressing these concerns, the ERP search team and the IS team realized that the process of implementing an ERP would push us to work and become familiar with our databases (reference files and transaction files). We knew that if we could discipline ourselves to make the data "clean," it would be much easier to move to another system if we had to. As an additional safeguard, we also negotiated an agreement to have the source code put in a bank account in case we needed it if TTW folded. While none of those fears turned out to be reality, such precautions are always wise. Ultimately, we decided it was more important to select a tool that fully reflected our needs (Win-Man had all the necessary modules and functionality) rather than deal with a larger company with a tool that had a function we might never need. In essence, this is similar to the process of selecting capital equipment for the shop floor in a lean environment. You find the tool that will perform the specific function needed for a specific manufacturing work cell and stay away from "flexible" equipment that can perform any type of work but includes extra features that you will never use.

Although there are some advantages to using the big industry standard tools, a mid-sized company normally does not need the power or scalability they provide. At the end of the day, what matters is what the ERP does, not how it does it. This philosophy reflects IS guiding principle #1, *Automate only if it is easier and faster than manually doing things*, which has an additional caveat: It is better to adapt technology that supports your culture and processes than to change things for the sake of technology or speed. In our case, we engaged the end users to evaluate and select the best ERP product that could reliably support their needs as well as deliver on our base product definition for technology and business preferences. Once we had the right product, we were confident that we could manage the rest of it. The lean lesson here is that concerns are not an obstacle to progress but an opportunity to develop possible alternatives to deal with the unexpected. Adapt and move on.

Managing Your ERP—Implementing a Vanilla Version vs. Customizing

When you begin implementing your ERP, you have a choice: Are you going to manage your ERP, or is your ERP going to manage you? That probably isn't a fair or polite way to ask the question, but it is a question that you must consider when you weigh your implementation options. Specifically, you will have to decide whether to install the vanilla version of the tool and fit your business processes to the tool or customize the ERP to make the tool fit your business process. The answer depends on how much you want to customize. You can go from 0 percent to 110 percent and anywhere in between. The good news is that there is no wrong answer as long as you understand what your choice means and are dedicated to supporting that choice.

If you are an IT manager, you might decide to go with the vanilla approach of 0 percent customization. Your system upgrades will be much easier, the vendor documentation will remain accurate, and you can give it directly to the user community. Implementation itself will be quick and easy. Moreover, the IT staff or management won't have to field questions such as, "Can we change this?" or "Why can't we do that?" Everyone will understand that what the tool offers is what is available. This approach can work because core business dynamics and transactions are more similar than not, even across different industries. Obviously, some ERP tools will be better suited than others for your business, but ERP developers design their tool to accommodate a broad range of customers. So going the vanilla route is a viable approach.

At Lantech, we chose to manage our ERP wherever we found significant value, which means we decided to customize even prior to our final selection. When you consider customizing your ERP, you have to deal with the same issues that make the vanilla approach cost effective. One thing that you must take into consideration is that customizing will affect the time and effort it takes to implement your ERP and, as a rule, will delay the "go live" date. That means you need to factor in additional resources and time when preparing for the implementation and lost efficiency the ERP would have given you during the delayed time frame. In addition, the customizing has to be done by someone and that someone has to be paid.

The Lantech team prioritized the changes we felt were needed to WinMan and then found a way to control the customization costs. We also scheduled an aggressive but realistic go live date. Any customizations that weren't completed by the go live date was done later or not done at all. This underscores a point already made above: Most ERPs will support most of your business processes; you just have to decide how important each change is and how much time and money you are willing to pay for the changes you want. You may find that some changes (i.e., some customization) are not worth the bother.

One important cost consideration is how effectively the vendor will support your customizations and future upgrades. The answer to this question could change your ERP selection and will certainly influence how you think about customizing. When Duane provided some ERP consulting for a Lantech partner that was implementing a different ERP system, the ERP vendor was willing to support some customizations in upgrades, but some would have to be re-created *after* each upgrade. That meant the company would have to limit its customizations, never upgrade, or accept significant pain and disruption as a part of each upgrade. None of these options is very attractive.

Lantech had a bit of luck with this issue of customization. During implementation, which is actually too late in the process, we asked TTW how it would support our changes. The company said it could and would work with us—and delivered! As we got more involved in TTW support and began to understand its customization structure, we found it quite flexible and workable. There have been glitches, which always take time to fix, but overall, the partnership between Lantech and TTW has worked very well.

Customizing ERP after Implementation

In a perfect world, you would expect to install your perfect system and your employees would go about performing their processes happily ever after. But we all know that this level of perfection is elusive and not easily achieved. Your customers, employees, business needs, and business processes change. When this happens, your ERP system might also have to change, and you will need to review your attitude about customizing. All the cost issues and constraints that were a part of both the vanilla and customized implementation still apply, but there is a new factor to consider. You have to decide *how much* you want to change or whether you want to change at all. This is a valid option. It would mean less training, fixed documentation, and no development costs, and if you made a reasonable choice to begin with, your ERP will support your business without changes or improvements. On the other hand, you can never forget that continuous improvement requires constant adaptation to changing circumstances and you will need to work hand-in-hand with the lean environment to remove wastes from your processes and systems. Running an information system that is not sufficiently adaptable will prevent you from removing waste and, over time, will create additional waste.

Lantech is committed to making its ERP tools support the changes we know will occur in our business. Even after implementation, we continue to customize our ERP and we customize it a lot. For most of the past eleven years, we have kept one or two programmers on staff to review and make changes to our ERP, and we are content that our model adds value and decreases cost. In connection with this, we apply the same basic continuous improvement approach to IS that we apply to manufacturing. For example, in our most advanced lean production lines, we look to remove seconds from the manufacturing process. In our most lean IT processes, we look for keystrokes to eliminate. In our still developing production lines, we look for minutes or hours to remove from the process. In some areas, we apply IS applications with the goal of eliminating or automating entire sequences of a process.

It is important to remember that lean is not just about eliminating wastes; it is sometimes about adding useful things. For instance, we sometimes add steps to the manufacturing process to assure quality in downstream processes and to satisfy the end customer. Likewise, we occasionally add steps to the IS processes, collecting additional data in order to assure quality and service. Additional up-front data collection ensures that all information you add to the information system is correct the first time, which significantly reduces customer disappointment, rework, and cross-checking within the business process later down-stream.

Common wisdom may suggest that you are limited as to the number of improvements you can make in any given area, but when continuous improvement is a constant across the organization, you continually find ways to improve last month's improvements. For example, a change in sales can spark an idea in purchasing that will suggest an improvement in engineering. The change in engineering will domino to an improvement in how to create equipment manuals, and the improved manuals will drive a change in the sales process, where the improvement cycle originated.

At Lantech, we change and improve our ERP every day. In the process, we gain new toolsets (or learn new tricks), especially relating to integration of WinMan to other applications like Word, Excel, and AutoCAD. Furthermore, because we add IT resources and willingly make changes, our user community now knows that no request is too outlandish to suggest. Some ideas are obviously too outlandish to consider seriously, but to generate good ideas among your employees you

"Once and Be Done"

The BPK team discovered that when an order was entered into the IT system by a fairly rote process that did not include any type of technical checks, both engineering and manufacturing repeated the process of checking the order. After identifying this waste, the customer service division/department put a more highly trained technical person in the job of reviewing and entering orders so that he or she could fix them before releasing the order to the engineering and fulfillment processes. Because of the lean philosophy of continuous improvements, this particular improvement revealed that some orders were simple or presented limited choices and did not require such intense scrutiny. The IS team went back to the power of the ERP system and developed simple configuration tools to check these types of orders. This way, we achieved accurate technical choices while avoiding the need for order entry people with a lot of technical expertise and reduced our costs. Once we had these up-front reviews of the technical aspects of the order in place, the order could flow through the fulfillment process without further checking and rework delays. By adding time up front, we achieved higher quality and fewer delays later. The entire process reflects IS guiding principle #10, *Capture information once and be done.*

"Once and be done" is our motto, principle, and philosophy, and we try to apply it to all aspects of our business. When we move material in manufacturing, we move it from where it is to where it needs to be for the next part of the manufacturing process. We don't store it on some shelf or double handle it by moving it from the shelf to the next work area when needed. Such maneuverings are the third and fourth deadly wastes: *Conveyance* or unnecessary transportation and *overprocessing or incorrect processing.* It is equally wasteful to double handle, or double enter, information, and this underscores the importance of IS guiding principle #7, *Keystrokes matter to power users*. Eliminating each keystroke, repetitive function, and double entries increases productivity and improves training.

There is a specific point in time when certain information is available, and there is a specific point in time when the information is needed. With this in mind, a company needs to review its business processes against the functionality of its ERP to determine when and what information is picked up and added. Whenever you add information, make sure everyone downstream has access to it without having to search for it without requesting that it be entered again. Do it once and be done!

have to encourage *all* ideas. Brainstorming in kaizen events is an excellent way to do this. So is having a "nothing is off limits" policy. Both result in a plentiful flow of good ideas and lay the groundwork for following IS guiding principle #4, *Nothing lasts forever*. As mentioned above, your business or customer will always change. It follows that your software or hardware will also change. In lieu of a perfect IT world, adaptability is your best competitive advantage.

The Power of Training and Keeping Programmers on Staff

A company could choose to route all its requests for customization and improvements to its ERP provider rather than incur the expense of maintaining a permanent programming staff. However, it may be shortsighted to consider only the cost of "resource overhead." For example, for most major ERP applications, the provider requires that you submit your changes and suggestions through its bureaucratic evaluation process. These suggestions can fall between the cracks, or worse, the provider will tell you up front that the cost of customization is more than you can afford. This is why a company needs to consider the total array of costs for system development, customization, and maintenance when selecting its ERP system. Alongside the normal questions about version upgrade frequency should be questions about who, when, and how much the provider will support the customizations. TTW and WinMan may be an exception to the rule in that they have always been very responsive to our requests for improving and implementing our ideas into the standard programs. Even though their costs are reasonable, the turnaround time for minor changes can take a day or two. By having its own programmers on staff, Lantech can move quickly to incorporate and easily test any kind of change, making the cost of maintaining a permanent IS staff much less of an overhead cost issue.

If you do choose to use programmers to maintain, upgrade, and customize your ERP, then you need to consider carefully whom you hire and train. We hired three different programmers over a two-year period, and though they were competent enough as programmers, they required lengthy and detailed instructions before mastering what to program and understanding how it was important to the business. The time and cost of training these programmers in Lantech business processes and database management was considerable. We tried a different approach—train our own business people. It soon became apparent that teaching business people to program rather than teaching technical people about the lean business was easier, faster, and wiser—a key breakthrough. As of this writing, about a third of the people we have on IS support do not have systems background per se, but they do have an interest in information systems, want to program, and know our business. Our suggestion is to develop your resources internally, training current employees with four to five years' experience. Training your workforce is both a common sense investment and a learning organizational approach. You are mentoring your employees to share, grow, and adapt. In turn, they are continually learning new skills. New knowledge and capabilities, as well as standardizing the work processes, assures quality work and continuous improvement.

Lantech's programmer-mentoring journey began with Duane Jones, whose background was in manufacturing with experience in purchasing, engineering, and sales. The ERP we chose had a different database and programming language from that used in the old network, but Duane was determined to learn it and use it. He was the first nontechnical person to learn to program from our first programmer, Steve Akers, with help from TTW associates Nick Jacobs, Scott Wilkinson, and Joe Wilkinson. Duane soon found that he loved the program and the programming, and interaction with the vendor grew from there. Duane understood Lantech's business requirements and was able to take verbal requests and turn them into system improvements without extensive interviewing, documenting, and flowcharting. Later, Duane trained three other associates in programming and database management, and within two months, each was able to maintain and manage small to medium complex system changes. Within six to nine months, they could develop and maintain complex applications.

Quick Training and Low Turnover

Lantech can now take employees with a business background with no programming experience but an interest in learning a programming skill, and make them productive in small jobs within a month or two. In three or four months, these individuals are handling and working with end users. When you consider the cost of hiring external people with technical backgrounds, who may only stay with your company one or two years, you realize the retraining activity and cost is too much. The loyalty in the group is high and the understanding of business is also high. The cycle time of projects becomes very short because the IS people understand lean strategy and work with users to get them exactly what they need in a new program.

The authors suspect that professionally trained IT professionals would disagree, but from our experience, it is easier for a person with a business background to learn programming than it is for a programmer to learn business. For a lean business, the IT professional has an added hurdle: not understanding lean. Once we established clear technological and business preferences criteria to define the type of ERP product for our company, our lean philosophy directed us to invite our end or system users review to select it. From there it was a matter of working with our provider to help support our lean environment through customization, training, and continuous improvement. It can be that simple.

The next chapter discusses how Lantech uses the kanban process to manage inventory and how it aligned and integrated ERP to support the lean shop. To continue with the preparation for and implementation of ERP, the reader can jump to Chapter 7, *Mission to Go Live—Building Teams and Overcoming Barriers*, where we pick up with the formation of the BPK team and its transformation into the ERP search team, and finally, the implementation/Wizard team.

CHAPTER 5

Kanban: Reducing Inventory and Managing Pull with Suppliers

CONTINUOUS IMPROVEMENT IS A PHILOSOPHY that naturally extends to delivering your product. At Lantech, the various kaizen teams are constantly reviewing how to improve the quality and cost of manufacturing, as well as how to deliver value to the customer. That means we change our product on a regular basis, whether it is replacing Part A with Part B, improving Part A, or combining Part A and Part B into a single component. Part of the improvement process includes determining the cost of the change. One aspect of that calculation is the impact of the change on the inventory on hand, and thus, one continuous improvement focus is reducing inventory on hand.

One important goal for a lean manufacturing company is the mandatory effort to reduce inventory. To approach the goal of one-piece flow you need to turn inventory rapidly through frequent deliveries of small lot sizes. Lantech uses JIT education as part of each kaizen event, and then follows up with additional courses to help employees accomplish this. For the first few years, learning about lean was also part of our new employee orientation. After implementing our initial cell via kaizen, we continued to use kaizen events and tools such as 5S and total productive maintenance (TPM) to improve those areas with the greatest barriers to improvement. We also continued to reinforce lean thinking.

This chapter reviews some of the major operational improvements and savings you will gain by using kanban externally with your suppliers to manage your pull system with less inventory. Many readers may be familiar with kanban, which may already be part of their company's operations. Our goal here is to discuss the specific benefits of kanban, working with your suppliers to support it, aligning your IS accordingly, and the benefits of managing less inventory. Because kanban is such an important tool to lean manufacturing, it is important to understand that your kanban efforts are more likely to succeed if you have already some lean elements (for example, TPM and JIT training) in your manufacturing process. Readers who are not familiar with implementing kanban in a lean environment might want to consult one or more books on the subject.[1]

Kanban Basics

Kanban is a Japanese word that means card, ticket, sign, or signboard. Like most lean companies, Lantech adopted kanban for its lean manufacturing process. For us, kanban evolved from being a simple procurement method into 1) a system process, 2) a system integration of JIT with our suppliers and, 3) an overall lean philosophy. This makes sense, because kanban operates in a pull system (JIT) to manage the flow of pulling materials in production. As defined in principle 4 in Chapter 1, *pull uses a material replenishment system that is initiated by consumption—the upstream supplier doesn't produce anything unless the downstream customer signals a need.* That is, in a pull system, a process makes

---

1. Productivity Press has a few Shopfloor Series primers that are helpful, such as *Kanban for the Shopfloor* and *Just-in-Time for Operators and Kanban.*

more parts only when the next process withdraws (pulls) parts when needed from the earlier process. As explained in Chapter 3, pull begins with the final process based on the actual or expected customer orders, which determines takt time. The final process uses kanban to pull needed parts from the previous process or production stage, which pulls from the process or production stage before it, and so on. It is the kanban card that signals this need, acting as a direct form of communication located at the point where the communication is needed.

Stages of Going Lean at Lantech

Our evolution toward becoming lean began when we went to one-piece flow cellular manufacturing—arranging equipment, workstations, and people in a process sequence that supports the pull system of smoothly flowing materials and components with minimal delay. It was during this time that we also adopted our hoshin planning process (discussed in Chapter 7) in tandem with implementing cellular manufacturing. Then we began working on our business or office processes. As our lean manufacturing efforts hit barriers, we used lean tools like kanban, TPM, and 5S to address them. (5S is a methodology for sorting, straightening [set in order], shining, standardizing, and sustaining a productive work environment. TPM focuses on running machinery optimally, minimizing equipment breakdowns, and eliminating waste by implementing preventative, corrective, and autonomous maintenance, as well as mistake-proofing techniques.)

Simultaneously, we engaged the business process activities, beginning with order entry, accounting, engineering, purchasing (overlapping with kanban), spare parts, shipping, receiving, etc. We used multiple kaizen events in each area, making them more lean as we implemented new processes and tools. We developed lean internally, eliminating work in process (WIP), improving lead time, etc., before externally applying kanban with our suppliers.

Companies commonly use kanban as an internal signal to drive production between work areas and manage JIT internally, but Lantech uses kanban as an external supplier signaling system. (In our cellular manufacturing setup, the work itself is the signal.) The only internal kanban we use is for our monument (a monument is a component of the process that is not dedicated to one or few value streams). All the Lantech products use the same paint line; here, it is not cards but the carts that serve as a physical signal. Applying kanban pull techniques with your suppliers means establishing a cost-effective and open information system with real-time communication so that your suppliers have the flexibility to meet demand requirements while keeping their own costs down. In other words, you want to use kanban to synchronize your suppliers to your customer demand. A key factor in achieving this is having clear and consistent communication with your suppliers, and this means using the same techniques, tools, and terminology.[2] This is possible only when your own "lean" house is in order.

Benefits of Less Inventory

There are numerous financial, legal, and operational reasons why you have to maintain some control and audits over what inventory you have and where it is located. The degree and complexity of those controls can vary from company to company and is often dictated by the kind of product a company produces. In any case, a kanban system eliminates inventory, which immediately helps you in four ways:

1. *Keeping track of smaller inventories frees time and money.* Less inventory means you will spend less energy and fewer resources on counting and recording and thus have more time for activities that directly impact your customer, company goals, and profit.

---

2. A very useful book that deals with kanban for suppliers is *Kanban for the Supply Chain* by Stephen Cimorelli (Productivity Press, 2006).

2. *Producing smaller inventories means you are not storing goods the customer may not want.* You will not be burdened with a stash of products the customer no longer wants or products that have become obsolete. You will also eliminate over-staffing (you won't need people who create these excess products), and you will avoid reworking products that are no longer profitable.

3. *Fewer damaged goods and increased storage.* With fewer goods, there are obviously fewer damaged goods. You will also have lower transportation costs, and, most important, you will have the use of space that is no longer being filled with excess inventory.

4. *Managing smaller inventories maximizes flexibility to make changes.* Because you will spend less time tracking and analyzing the costs of the inventory, you will have more flexibility in making engineering changes and will be able to proceed more quickly with your product development.

There is a positive calculated financial reason to minimize your inventory. When Lantech was operating in a traditional MRP environment, we thought in terms of weeks instead of days, and we produced our product in two levels of subassemblies and one level of finished goods. The example in Table 5-1 illustrates how the lean process takes $1,000 worth of purchased inventory to build one day's supply of shippable products and takes $300 of direct labor to produce one day's supply of shippable products. Lantech now keeps one day's worth of inventory on the shelf and another day's inventory tied up in WIP and/or finished goods. That means $1,000 on the shelf, $1,000 in WIP, and $300 in labor, totaling $2,300 invested in inventory on any given day. When compared with our traditional MRP approach, the lean $2,300 is only 10 percent of $23,000. The bottom line is an inventory investment savings of $20,700.

Table 5-1. Comparison on Inventory Investment—Lean vs. MRP

Lean Process		Traditional MRP	
Inventory Level	Inventory Dollars	Inventory Level	Inventory Dollars
Purchased – one day	1,000	Purchased – one week	5,000
		First Subassembly material	5,000
		First Subassembly labor	500
		Second Sub-assembly material	5,000
		Second Sub-assembly labor	1,000
Final Assembly – one day	1,000	Final Assembly material	5,000
Final Assembly labor	300	Final Assembly labor	1,500
Total Dollars	2,300		23,000

What if you have $1 million invested in your inventory? Switching from traditional MRP to lean means you have nearly $900,000 available to invest in research, infrastructure, acquisition, or whatever you need to push your company ahead of the competition. This is not a simplistic, pie-in-the-sky example. A 90 percent savings is a very real possibility. Even if your company can pull off only a 50 percent savings, it is well worth the effort.

There is more to reducing inventory than making a decision to buy less. If a reduced inventory initiative stops work in your production line because you lack the required materials, you have obviously made a huge blunder, which could jeopardize customer satisfaction and profitability. The pull system is about making sure you buy the right thing at the right time and have enough of what you need when you need it. A traditional MRP will not get you there.

MRP Produces More Inventory, Less Flexibility

To understand this concept, consider how a standard MRP procurement process works. Someone in the purchasing department receives notification that material is required. This notification normally comes from an MRP-generated report. Depending on the nature of the company or the individual, this notification might be acted on immediately or automatically. On the other hand, the material procured or the notification itself might be scrutinized and analyzed before processing to ensure its validity.

Either action carries a cost. Purchasing automatically from MRP-generated reports can lead to excesses in inventory or shortages based on vagaries and inaccuracies in the system. Too much analyzing means carrying more staff.

In any event, you eventually send a purchase order to a supplier who must then go through internal processes and respond with a shipping date and price confirmation. Assuming the shipping date and prices are acceptable, the required item arrives in due time at your receiving dock. Normally, the receiving clerk will confirm that the correct item and quantity has been shipped. Possibly the receiving clerk or a member of the quality control team will inspect the item and confirm it is the correct version and meets required specifications before making out a receipt. The item now makes its way to an operational storage area and is eventually transferred (both physically and via system transaction) to the appropriate manufacturing area. If at this point you discover the item is defective, purchasing re-enters the picture, expediting a replacement for the required part and negotiating with the supplier for a credit.

The Negative Side of Too Much Inventory

When Lantech was organized around operational functions, the manufacturing division was introducing a new design that had been handed over from the research and development division. The manufacturing division was operating in a very traditional MRP mode at the time, and optimum costing of a new product required bulk purchasing of some components. Duane, who was coordinating engineering changes, received notice from R&D that three types of sprockets in inventory needed to be replaced by three new sprockets. He checked inventory and then reported to the manufacturing division vice president that the change was going to cost the company $20,000 in obsolescence. The manufacturing division vice president then advised the vice president of R&D of the consequences of not consuming the inventory on hand, but R&D went through with the change immediately anyway. We kept the three sprockets on hand for a year or two in the vain hope of using them somewhere, but in the end, we tossed $20,000 worth of sprockets into the dumpster.

Scrapping such items or returning them to the vendor with a restocking fee carries a direct cost to the bottom line, but delaying any requested changes from R&D means you must keep products from shipping without the benefit of product improvement. Obviously, when you have less inventory on hand or committed, making changes will reduce your loss. Either way, the choice has a cost and the implication of that choice is a short-term benefit for the company or an immediate and ongoing benefit to the customer.

Lantech's development process when introducing new or changing products is now an integral part of an ongoing effort to reduce inventory and minimize losses.

Meanwhile, the vendor generates an invoice and sends it to your accounts payable department. The invoice is sorted by vendor and date and compared with shipping receipts to confirm the item was actually delivered. Next, accounts payable compares the terms with the purchase order for consistency and then authorizes payment for commerce to proceed.

Kanban is a far, far better way to approach inventory replenishment.

The Kanban Process Begins to Open Doors

The kanban method assures delivery on two essential lean points: reduced inventory (wastes) and simplicity in procurement (pull system). It begins with determining the minimum amount of inventory required to meet production needs per day, which is determined by customer orders. You use kanban to make sure you have only what you need available each day. Lantech has had several kanban process versions over the years. Duane was a co-captain with a factory team leader on the team that put in the first kanban process, and he has participated in other initiatives over the years.

Unlike the MRP process, the kanban process begins with purchasing, whose main role is to negotiate with the supplier to an agreed upon fixed price and turnaround time. Purchasing communicates this supplier information to manufacturing, which determines how much inventory it wants on hand and what quantities (bundles) the supplier should deliver. Table 5-2 shows an example of the calculation we use to determine inventory and the number of kanban cards needed to communicate this:

Manufacturing then creates a kanban card, about the size of an index card, which contains the required information as shown in Figure 5-1.

Lantech made an addition to the kanban card that demonstrates the all-encompassing focus on continuous improvement. The material handlers decided it would be helpful to place an image of any given part on the back of the kanban card. This would make it easy for new associates to identify parts and help long-term associates identify new parts. Without asking advice or permission, the material handlers

Table 5-2. Typical Calculation to Determine Inventory and Number of Kanban Cards

Kanban Formula	Amounts
The number of parts required per unit	5
× the number of units built per day	10
=	
Total parts required per day	50
× part lead time in days	4
=	
Total parts required during lead-time cycle	200
+ Safety Stock (one day's requirement)	50
=	
Total parts in cycle	250
/ Preferred Qty per shipment	25
=	
Number of kanban cards	10

began adding part images to the kanban cards. This is now part of their standard work.

Once all required information is entered on the kanban card, the inventory on hand is then bundled in quantities corresponding to the quantity specified on the card, and the card is attached to the bundles. (If there is material left over, with no kanban card attached, that inventory is used first, and this continues until you reach the desired level of inventory that you want to maintain.) When the material handler or manufacturing associate opens a bundle of items with a kanban card attached, they immediately place that kanban card in a nearby kanban card collection container. In a single manufacturing area of 15,000 square feet, Lantech has 12 collection points, conveniently spread out to make sure it is easy for associates to find and deposit the kanban cards. Through the course of the day or at the end

Figure 5-1. Typical Lantech Kanban Card

of the day, a material handler (often called a water spider in lean companies) collects the kanban cards.

In our early lean initiatives, we sorted the kanban cards by supplier and then copied four onto a single page. The assembled pages were then faxed to the appropriate supplier. While this may sound a bit archaic—

and it is—it worked quite well and cost next to nothing. Today, however, Lantech material handlers scan the kanban cards into our ERP system to confirm that none have been lost or skipped in the process.

The next step is to send our kanban card requests to our suppliers (by fax or by e-mail) once each day or night. Following the preagreement arrangements made with purchasing, the supplier then ships the required quantity of items on the required date. The items arrive at our receiving dock bundled in the appropriate quantities with the appropriate kanban information attached. The receiving team then scans the bar code or keys in the bar code number. Each kanban item should be labeled with the required manufacturing location and shelf ID so a handler can take the item exactly where it belongs without any intermediary handling or stocking. Most companies are familiar with or use some form of bar coding, which is an excellent example of IS guiding principle #7, *Keystrokes matter to power users*. Kanban with suppliers creates a significant increase in receiving activity, making every keystroke matter.

That is kanban in a nutshell and in its simplest form. In lean thinking, there is no need to wait or design a perfect solution for your system processes. You use what you have. Forget about waiting for the financial investment or best possible ROI; just do it! Get your employees involved to implement what you can as soon as you can. Redesigning your work process around kanban to create flow will produce the right results.

Kanban Reduces Inventory, Eliminates Waste, and Improves Savings

Let's review the new roles of purchasing, manufacturing, receiving, and material handling to see the improvements at this point in the process. Purchasing is no longer engaged in the day-to-day loop of inventory acquisition and can now focus on performing the initial negotiation and participate in a monitoring process. Freed from the repetitive daily transactions, purchasing can also engage in activities like researching new suppliers or implementing and tracking cost-reduction initiatives. Moreover, once your suppliers have adopted kanban, you may find that your current purchasing group will be overstaffed, which means you can transfer their expertise elsewhere in the company. Most purchasing departments spend 70 percent of their time on purchasing transactions, with only 30 percent going to analysis or strategy. When the effort on transactions is reduced from kanban and other waste elimination activities, purchasing expertise can focus on materials strategy, one of the greatest expenses in most companies and, generally, one of the least evaluated from a strategy perspective.

Manufacturing is effectively in direct contact with the supplier—there is no go-between or middleman to slow things down. The supplier receives the material requirements on the same day they are recognized—real material requirements, not projected requirements, not possible requirements. In other words, manufacturing buys material it knows it is going to use and use relatively quickly.

Receiving now processes receipts more quickly: Scan (or key) and Enter. You also reduce the physical process. You no longer need to verify the quantity of most kanban receipts (though you may do spot checks). Above all, while this may sound a little strange, you don't need to worry about inspecting an item from a quality perspective anymore. We'll explain how and why this works below.

Back in the early 1990s, Lantech was still receiving and storing all material in a central parts crib. The material handlers would take the material off the shelf and transfer it to the manufacturing area as required. Then the manufacturing area handled the material at least once more to move it to the actual work area. Because the kanban card carries the exact manufacturing location and shelf ID, the handler can now take the parts bin and place every item in the right place the first time. We have completely eliminated the central parts crib and redeployed the staff that supported it.

The big question at this point is whether we have reduced inventory. After all, Table 5-2 shows 10 kanban cards for a quantity of 25 each for a total of 250 items in stock. But once our kanban process was in full swing, the norm became 2 to 4 cards or bundles on the shelf at any given time, with the other 6 or 7 cards moving between the manufacturing location and the supplier. We are so confident in the process that when we introduce new items, even though we may have 250 items in the full cycle, we allow shelf space for only 50 to 100 of those new items. That is all we will ever have on the shelf.

A purist may observe that we seem to be hedging our bets by including safety stock in our kanban calculation, and that would be a correct assumption. Continuous improvement *aims* for the lean principle of perfection, which does not mean the same as *achieving* perfection. Lean thinking assumes you will need some buffer and allows for human imperfection, as well as for mechanical glitches or even nature. Recall the discussion on takt time in Chapter 3; you want to produce products that are in sync with customer orders and to ship them as soon as the products are completed. Then consider potential obstacles that might arise. Sometimes suppliers are late, sometimes parts are defective, and sometimes we forget to send the signal to the supplier on time. In such instances, safety stock keeps the manufacturing process from missing a beat. We like to ship product on time, and our customers like us to ship on time. We think a little safety stock is a healthy balance to assure the deliverable to the customer. The objective is to drive your inventory to the lowest level required to deliver value to the customer.

So, yes, we have used kanban to reduce inventory. Moreover, we have also reduced work in material handling and receiving. Some MRP users might argue that although we have simplified the receiving process, we have actually increased the number of transactions required, and that is also true. Under a standard MRP methodology, we might receive 100 of an item once a week. Under kanban, we receive 10 of an item 10 times a week—ten transactions versus one transaction. But even if we have increased the workload in receiving, we still have decreased the time and expense in purchasing and material handling—and reduced inventory.

Kanban's pull system has an additional benefit: the ergonomics gain of working with smaller and lighter loads. Because the loads are lighter, we don't need forklifts to deliver pallets of parts to manufacturing. Instead, we use waist-high pushcarts, which means less bending over in receiving and, when the carts are unloaded, in manufacturing. Enhanced safety is an important and positive gain, as well as a foundational lean goal.

Integrating the Kanban Process into the ERP System

Once you have kanban in place, the challenge is to use your ERP system to complement the new process. This means simplifying the IS process. When Lantech first began using kanban, it was only an internal process, and we maintained blanket purchase orders in a traditional MRP system to support the kanban flow. Consequently, the receiving process for kanban receipts was identical to standard receiving. If we had stayed with that MRP system, however, the increased work in receiving would have been questionable and may have required increased staffing. Therefore, once we implemented the process of kanban procurement, we began to tackle the IS aspects of supporting it.

We implemented WinMan in 1995, and a key discussion point before and during implementation was how to address the IS integration of the kanban process into our ERP. We met with Joe Wilkinson, the founder of TTW, and in a matter of hours, we had talked through the kanban process, IS, ERP, and ways and means to bring all three together in a meaningful and productive way. It wasn't long before we were able to visualize how easily kanban could be used as part of an integrated ERP system. All it took was a single transaction of a single step—providing the material requirement to the supplier—and another single transaction of a single step—getting that item into our inventory in the precise location and shelf where it is required. From here, it was a matter of transitioning from manually faxing the kanban cards to sending the data electronically to our suppliers. How we send the information to suppliers—fax, e-mail text attachments, spread-sheets—is, to some degree, at their discretion. It is all straightforward, and after some acquisitions and general interest over the years, we have had an opportunity to review several other ERP systems and have yet to see any that are as integrated and streamlined to the kanban process.

One side effect to using kanban was that the number of inventory receipt transactions increased substantially. Even with WinMan and a simplified kanban receiving process, there was still a lot of scanning and keyboarding in receiving. To reduce of the effects of this, we turned to the IS team and our ERP system and developed a simplified electronic receiving process. Lantech's major suppliers now provide a standardized Excel spreadsheet of all items per each delivery. With only a few clicks of the mouse our ERP systems scans, verifies, and receives all the items in the spreadsheet. We know there are more sophisticated methods available (EDI, wireless bar coding, etc.), and we may further investigate these solutions some day. For now, our spreadsheet solution uses existing tools that are already familiar both to our users and suppliers. The only "real" cost was about four hours of programming time. The solution highlights a core kaizen principle: *Creativity before capital.*

The broader lesson is that you should not hesitate to implement kanban just because you don't have an ERP "kanban" module in place. Moreover, you don't have to have a system linking your kanban cards to your ERP. You can begin using kanban on the shop floor, as we did, and then create blanket purchase orders in whatever ERP system you have. Meanwhile, you can create your kanban cards in Word or Excel or with crayons and construction paper. Then send your kanban cards to your supplier; receiving receives them against the blanket purchase orders. The benefits derived from the significant inventory reduction of kanban are worth making the effort by whatever means you can.

Creating Self-Billing Invoices

Lantech's kanban process from a procurement and operational perspective was a complete success. Inventory and material handling was down and overall effort and costs were down. But there was one aspect of kanban that was causing a problem: We were receiving an item ten times a week instead of once a week. Because of this, our accounts payable associate, Janis Riddle, was processing ten invoices a week instead of one!

As our use of kanban increased across multiple product lines, Janis's workload increased to the point that we occasionally pulled a resource from some other area just to open envelopes and sort the invoices that were pouring in. The savings in the kanban process was so substantial that adding another person in accounting was a reasonable solution, but we had stopped being reasonable people. We wanted something better. Again, we turned to TTW for a solution.

Joe Wilkinson reviewed the problem of our mounting workload in accounts payable with Janis Riddle and Cathy Taylor in accounting, and they brainstormed an operational concept solution and a system program we now call Self-Billing Invoices (SBI). This solution entailed negotiating with our suppliers, particularly the ones who were heavily involved in the kanban process, to stop sending us any more invoices. Instead, we would pay them upon receipt of their shipments. In addition, TTW created a program that allowed Janis to review all the receipts for a given supplier for the previous day, point and click to exclude a few exceptions, mark all the rest for payment, and voilá—the checks could go out. A task that required a person and a half each day was reduced by more than half, Janis was easily able to process all of AP in less than a day. As a result, Janis had time to learn other tasks and now spends a portion of her day working in accounts receivable.

We could have stopped there and congratulated ourselves on a job well done, but Janis began noticing something new in her process. She had always focused on doing extra work to locate and pay early those suppliers who offered a discount for early payment. Now she could easily pay any and every supplier early if needed. So purchasing began pushing for an early payment discount with all suppliers, especially with those who were part of the kanban process. In 1997, we were averaging $12,173 a month savings in early payment discounts. In 2002, we averaged $25,051 a month savings in early payment discounts—that was an additional savings of $154,536 annually. In 2005, we saved $445,000. We saved not only because our ERP system was configured to pay suppliers quickly and easily, but because more of our suppliers had an incentive to offer discounts in order to participate in the kanban process. They, too, were freed from the invoicing process, and early payment improved their cash flow.

Kanban Builds Stronger Supplier Relationships

Some readers may argue, "Our suppliers would never do that," and they would be right. Not all suppliers will work with the kanban process. Sadly, some suppliers who chose this path no longer work with Lantech. The kanban principle was too valuable for us to ignore, so we found (and continue to seek out) replacement suppliers who will participate in kanban.

Another reservation might be, "We don't trust our suppliers that much." This is also a good point. For the front-to-back process to work well, you and your supplier need a relationship of trust. But the kanban process provides ways to help build and ensure that trust. Earlier in this chapter, we mentioned that we don't confirm quantity or quality on kanban receipts. An unscrupulous supplier could take advantage of us on this point and feel confident of getting away with it because we pay based on receipt. We realized early on that there seemed to be no checks in the system, so we built in some.

Part of the agreement with suppliers who join us in the kanban process is that we do not waste time fussing over quality issues. If a kanban part is defective, we take a credit against the supplier's account and put the part back on the next truck. We don't argue about it. We don't even discuss it. We take the credit immediately, and the supplier does not get paid for the defective part. This policy ensures that we never eat the cost; the supplier does, and most see that as an incentive not to send Lantech defective parts.

Another potential problem in the process is that suppliers may undership on quantity. This can and does happen. Lantech has never had an instance of a supplier deliberately shipping too little, but there have been accidents. The kanban process makes this less of a problem than you would think. To begin with, because we receive smaller quantities with kanban, it is easy to verify that the correct quantity has been shipped. Moreover, we don't keep much inventory on hand in any given manufacturing location. We keep just enough to finish the day and start tomorrow. Remember, achieving one-piece flow in a lean environment means rapidly turning inventory through frequent deliveries of small lot sizes. A reasonably trained associate with experience regarding the parts in a given area can easily see when we might be running short. And because we keep so little inventory, it doesn't take long to backtrack and find out where the shortage may have occurred. We can't always confirm a supplier shorted us, but because we do have good relationships with our suppliers, we can mention the undershipment issues to them and that usually takes care of the problem. After all, we both want to succeed and we both recognize that one partner's success cannot be achieved in the long term at the other's expense. When we work together to monitor and correct issues that arise, we both win.

In *Real Numbers,* one of the Lean Accounting Principles is *If the cost to control is greater than the cost of the risk, take the risk.* In lean thinking, the strength of any good supply chain management is to respect your network of suppliers, share business goals on mutual trust and respect, and work with and encourage suppliers to apply lean principles, in this case, kanban. With this in place, everyone responsible for implementing and maintaining the kanban systems understands the role of the supplier.

Inventory Accuracy Is Less Critical with a Kanban System

There is another curious twist to kanban that we perceive in a positive light: *Kanban tends to make inventory accuracy less critical.* Some inventory control managers might not care for this twist, and some lean consultants don't even understand it. But if you think about, it makes perfect sense. Kanban works to make sure you always have what you need. If a part is damaged and an associate throws it in the garbage without recording it in the system, then the inventory listed in the computer is off. Nevertheless, the kanban process on the shop floor still ensures you physically have what you need. If the Bill of Material is inaccurate and issues too much in the computer records or ignores a part actually being used, the kanban process still makes sure you have what you need and only what you need regardless of what your ERP system may be showing. We began to see the logic of this when we started comparing our manufacturing inventory with our spare parts inventory.

In our ERP system, when the customer orders a spare part, the system checks our spare parts inventory. If the system shows the part is available, the part is triggered to be shipped and the customer (if required) is notified immediately. Inventory accuracy matters in this area—both for the expensive parts and for the inexpensive parts. We cannot afford to tell a customer a part will ship the same day and then

discover we really don't have it. And we don't want to have an acciden-
tal build of a spare part that is only used as a spare part; it's too easy to
get caught with a lot of obsolescence. The sequence below shows what
happens next and how the kanban provides its own safeguards. So do
our people.

In the manufacturing inventory, the associate takes the kanban
item off the shelf and uses it. If it is time, he turns in the kanban card
and more items are ordered. It doesn't matter to him if the ERP system
says we have 1 or 1,000. He has the one he needs and he knows more
are on order because kanban is a manual and visual process.

The spare parts inventory associates, however, spend a part of each
day counting and verifying their inventory, because in their area it does
matter. The manufacturing associates count their inventory only once
a year because auditors require them to.

Don't get the impression that by paying less attention to inventory accuracy we are ignoring the root causes of inventory inaccu-
racy. We train associates to take proper measures when parts are
faulty or misplaced, and provide them with straightforward tools
(stock adjustment, stock rejection, stock transfer, etc.) to record the
damage or loss of a part and why the damage or loss occurred. In
addition, we have developed some sophisticated tools for researching
our Bills of Materials (BOMs) to make sure they properly reflect our
equipment as built. We have numerous options for exploding a
BOM, summarized, full detail, purchased parts only, raw material
only, assemblies only, etc. We also developed a BOM implosion tool.
After exploding the top level of a BOM, we can pick any item at any
level and discretely review its relationship within the multilevel
structure. Inventory impacts notwithstanding, we understand the
obligation to after-market support.

Anyone with a little inventory experience will recognize there are
shades of gray involved, but the bottom line is that we now spend a
lot less time counting inventory than we did before implementing

our kanban process. We have learned over the years that it actually takes a pretty competent person to do good cycle counts, and there are plenty of more productive tasks for a competent person to be doing than just counting.

Is kanban an end unto itself? We think it is. The reduced inventory alone is worth the effort. And then there is the fact that the kanban system manages flow within the framework of a JIT (pull) environment that provides flexibility and better relations with our suppliers. Moreover, when you tie a good kanban process into an integrated ERP system, more doors start to open and you begin to see improvements in purchasing, engineering, and accounting. You also reduce labor costs in most areas and foster creativity in others. Kanban gives your employees more time and energy and a fresh perspective so they can look at all your other business and system processes in a new light and help find ways for more improvements. To achieve this, you have to be willing to reshuffle your existing MRP, a subject covered in the next chapter.

CHAPTER 6

Reshuffling MRP to Align with Kanban and Lean

D UANE JONES HAS WORKED WITH FOUR DIFFERENT MRP systems over the last fifteen years and has reviewed twenty more. In the process, he has found that on any given day, the acronym "MRP" means different things to different people. The exact meaning of an MRP system, apparently, is a little nebulous, and those people who use the system have their own unique interpretation of its nature and function. This book, for example, defines MRP in light of how Lantech has used it.

By now, the reader has a good understanding of an ERP system as an integrated computerized set of operations that ideally include every facet of every operation a company performs. MRP is usually a subset within the ERP system, though it sometimes is a stand-alone system with functionality limited to the MRP process. You can call the MRP module Material Resource Planning or Material Requirements Planning. In its most full-blown form, MRP is a program that determines what things you want to produce and when. It draws this information from the Sales Order Process, minimum stock-on-hand values, or various artificial means you use to tell the process to build a particular item. MRP then determines what raw material you need, what items you need to manufacture, what equipment you need, and what labor force you need.

Once this information is in place, MRP weighs the first two items against what raw material you already have, what you have on order, what you have already built, what you are building, what equipment you have, and what human resources you have available. In essence, the output of MRP is a schedule: Whether you manipulate your MRP system manually or electronically, your end product is a to-do list that suggests what you need to do and when you should do it in order to produce what you want when you want it.

The only real calculation MRP performs is to compare what you want to what you have, and this determines the resources you need to get product to the customer. Most MRP processes can probably be configured to place purchase orders or notify employees of starting times and tasks automatically; in our opinion, however, running a company with a fully automated MRP process is too risky.

To be fair, a great many companies do take the MRP suggestions and act on them without too much review. If you have your supporting processes in place, MRP suggestions can be highly accurate. In the past, Lantech operated in this manner and it was a profitable arrangement, one that proved it is possible to run an operation successfully with MRP driving core manufacturing functions. Our customers, however, only want to pay us for what they think our products are worth, so we had to find ways to cut costs to remain profitable, or more accurately, to become more profitable. The way we were using MRP at the time did not fully support this until we integrated our MRP system with our lean system.

Role of MRP in Lean

One result of Lantech's lean efforts was that it showed us how we should or should not use MRP. The first thing the BKP team dropped from our MRP was the labor force calculations. When we went to one-piece flow cellular manufacturing, scheduling and tracking labor became much simpler. In our pull environment, we calculated that our order entry rate for our Q300 product required us to build ten a day. Because our assembly line required ten associates to build ten machines a day, we scheduled ten associates to work on that line every day. We did not need a system-generated report to tell us we needed ten people nor did we need these people to record their work time in the system so that we knew they were working each day. The fact that the product was being loaded on the truck as scheduled was evidence enough.

You might question how we deploy our workforce effectively, without a capacity and requirement schedule. Lantech builds one machine at a time to customer order—what we have actually sold—and this puts our manufacturing people in sync with sales. If sales increase beyond the ten-a-day standard, manufacturing adds a couple of extra people to the line, redeploying the workload to accommodate the increased demand. Alternatively, manufacturing may decide to use the same ten associates who then work an extra two hours per day. The only critical point here is that manufacturing schedules labor hours based on actual sales, not on suggestions from an MRP-generated report. For Lantech, some fluctuation in the lead time is acceptable. For other companies, if the ability to produce to customer-demanded lead times is not possible, keeping some stock on hand may be necessary. Nonetheless, the scheduling process can be just as simple.

Some companies may be concerned that they cannot get accurate labor costs if they are not scheduling and tracking. The solution to this is simple: Know how many associates it takes to build your product, and you know the labor costs. At Lantech, it takes ten associates to build ten machines. Even if the labor on different machines varies, our prices are set. The variations in labor will never be severe enough to merit a price change (at least not without a review), so we don't have to worry about daily inputting and updating labor hours in an MRP system. Occasionally we like to have more details about a specific machine, but it is cheaper to deal with that machine on an exception basis rather than track every machine on the line.

Even in our pre-lean days, Lantech never tracked equipment capacity in any of its MRP systems. Many companies do this, but there is no significant value in scheduling or tracking the capacity of equipment with one-piece flow because the manufacturing flow dictates that you put equipment where it makes sense and use it when you need it. The machine remains idle when you don't need it because lean thinking does not involve trying to achieve 100 percent capacity use. In fact, this would be a sign of waste—producing things regardless of customer demand. If a company does have machinery that is at capacity, the theory of constraints (TOC) is an excellent method for optimizing the throughput of the organization, until either waste in the running of the machinery unlocks capacity, or additional equipment is available to meet customer demand.[1]

Before adopting one-piece flow, Lantech depended almost entirely on MRP. It was a material volume issue, plain and simple, to tell us when and what we should purchase. Implementing kanban changed all that, relegating MRP into a lesser role in terms of volume. Chapter 5 explained how to order and deliver kanban items outside of the normal purchasing process. You also exclude these items from the normal MRP process. Because we integrated our kanban process with the WinMan ERP system, we simply set a system flag to ignore all kanban items. As a result, no purchase orders were suggested and there weren't any to review. The material was always just-in-time.

Since implementing this MRP, over 90 percent of our material is being ordered and delivered without detailed management oversight, and we continue to maintain minimal inventory levels. In 2005, we

---

1. An excellent book for applying the theory of constrains is Eli Goldratt's, *The Goal.*

issued 9,274,879 items into WIP. Only 6.5 percent of those items were procured through the MRP process. For our highest volume product, the percentage was less than 3 percent.

The Pre-MRP Program

Lantech went from using a traditional MRP process for measuring labor capacity and procuring 100 percent of our material to using MRP for procuring less than 10 percent of our material. But that was only the beginning. We were several years into our relationship with TTW and using WinMan when many employees across the company realized that system modifications were often just a matter of making a request to the IS team. Although the IS team did not respond to every whim of every user, it did act upon requests that made sense and would enhance the business process. Today, many of our employees' ideas are incorporated into the standard WinMan product.

For example, the IS team received a request from the scheduling/purchasing teams about an MRP option to purchase items specific to a particular job. Duane and Jeanine Holden, one of the schedulers, typed up the specification for the process. Based on this, we developed a tool we call Pre-MRP, which we have continued to improve and expand over the years.

The core process of Pre-MRP is quite simple. The product line scheduler opens the program and enters the top-level part number for a machine to be built. The Pre-MRP program explodes the Bill of Material for that product down to just the purchase level. Naturally, we exclude all kanban items because they are going to be delivered via their own process. The scheduler is left with a shortlist of the nonkanban items, which are required to build the product in question. The Pre-MRP program lists the quantity on hand and current requirements for each item, as well as the various suppliers and costs and lead time. To purchase an item, the scheduler points and clicks items from the computer screen and sets a delivery date. The scheduler finalizes the process and sends out multiple purchase orders to various suppliers. The final step in the process is when the parts arrive at the dock door the day before manufacturing requires them, with a note attached to each one indicating the exact sales order and machine for which the item was purchased. The material handler takes the parts directly to the correct product line and places them with the other components that are needed for the specific job.

It is difficult to measure the productivity improvement we gained by using the Pre-MRP tool. What is certain is that it immediately improved communication by eliminating wastes, especially the deadly waste number one, overproducing information. The user can now retrieve information for just one order. Without this tool, the purchasing staff had to review daily standard MRP suggestions on which parts to buy and when to buy them, but had no knowledge of why they should buy them. Ultimately, they would either act blindly or call around until they found someone who did know. Now, schedulers, who have an intimate knowledge of their product and how critical the delivery is for each item, place purchase orders on the shop floor. The Pre-MRP tool reflects IS guiding principle #2, *Build commonality to increase visibility and access to information.* It provides visual management and control to the schedulers and purchasing department so that, with a few clicks they can make decisions without having to waste time looking for the right person to give them the right information. The tool also reinforces IS guiding principle #10, *Capture information once and be done*, especially because it allows users to capture quality information early in the process.

MRP Benefits

Kanban captures over 90 percent of our material, and individuals with specific product knowledge discretely purchase the balance. Theoretically, this makes it possible for Lantech to stop using the standard MRP process. But there is a good reason we still run the standard MRP process each weeknight: It still does well what it is supposed to do. It compares what we have on hand and on order with what we need and makes suggestions about what we should do. This in no way contradicts the premise that kanban eliminates the need for such suggestions. As anyone running a business knows, things outside the control and knowledge of the people who need to know can and do happen. When they do happen, MRP makes it easier to correct the results. The examples below illustrate this concept:

- *Damaged or scrapped goods*: You may have only one of an item in stock and it is damaged and scrapped, but the original scheduler who ordered the item believes it is in stock, available, and in good condition. MRP suggests ordering one more item.

- *Engineering Changes*: An engineering change takes place, but it is processed with incorrect notification. MRP will match and catch this error.

- *Cancelled Orders*: A customer can cancel an order.

- *Unexpected or Sudden Orders*: A customer in the field can require a part on short notice.

As this list shows, exceptions to the normal process will occur, and the standard MRP process will capture and report against those exceptions. In most cases, you can direct exception reports to the person who has the knowledge to respond most effectively.

MRP No Longer Manages You

At Lantech, MRP was once viewed as an indispensable but sometimes overbearing lifeline that issued suggestions that were to be followed to the letter. The company depended on the system's precision and accuracy to support it, and the system made sure everything was properly rigged and maintained. If the system had a problem, however, it could disrupt everything, sometimes with serious repercussions. Today,

MRP's role has changed. It no longer dictates what is to be done. Instead, it has been relegated to the role of a dependable safety net.

The company had several reasons for decreasing and toning down MRP's role. One of the most important of these was that the smallest of errors in MRP created assumptions that caused or inappropriately suggested "poor performance." One example will demonstrate the nature of the problems that surfaced because of this. Rick Norris was a good scheduler in our traditional MRP days and was very familiar with our product, options, sales forecast, and manufacturing capacity. One day he misread one of his reports and accidentally added into the manufacturing schedule ten expensive low-volume options. MRP ran and handed down instructions. Purchasing staff probably noticed the increase in the low-volume items, but the report said buy, so they bought. The machine and fabrication shops noticed a slight increase in the work order, but their schedule said build ten more, so they produced. The assembly team noticed the increase, but their incentive was to clock hours and so they followed the schedule and built the options. Rick did not discover the mistake in time to "stop the presses" and had to report the problem to a vice president who was understandably displeased by the news. Manufacturing was stuck with the items and had to store them for several months. During that time, the units trickled out one by one. Meanwhile, Rick waited and hoped there would be no significant engineering changes requiring rework.

Costly mistakes of this kind do happen, but the sequence of events above did not occur only because of Rick's initial error. It occurred because the MRP system had churned out a report that automatically told everybody else in the chain to do a job *without real knowledge of the customer or the real needs of the company*. Today, we buy something when a manufacturing associate pulls a kanban card to consumer material that needs to be replaced the next day or when a scheduler places a purchase order for a specific customer. If we cut a piece of steel or drill a single hole, the operator knows the name of the customer who is going to receive the final product.

We continue to use ERP to make our process more lean, but many of the functions we perform are now guided by kanban rather than by MRP. In making the shift, we have eliminated purchasing from most of the standard buying processes, freeing purchasing to manage the suppliers. For a time, purchasing still had responsibility for monitoring each kanban order and purchase order, which took tedious hours of collecting, collating, and annotating documents, not to mention the waste in waiting for information by phone, e-mails, or faxes. Using ERP, however, the IS team created a suite of programs in conjunction with standard Microsoft products to give our suppliers remote access. They can now check off the purchase orders they have received and list any exceptions to the delivery or price. We also capture and store this data electronically. In addition, suppliers can reprint purchase orders or have engineering drawings automatically e-mailed to them. Purchasing now only needs to follow up on the exceptions and fully owns the tool, providing all the training for the supply base. Reviewing this tool with one of our major suppliers showed that it improved the supplier's processes in the same way it had improved our own. It created a single point for checking data, which provided quicker communication and turnaround, a win–win proposition for all parties. The changeover is another example of IS guiding principle #11, *Use commonality to create an information highway.* Having your data properly organized enables structured input and access of that data from multiple points.

This is also a demonstration of IS guiding principle #13, *Huge data stores are easy to manipulate.* You should take every opportunity to collect any data that helps you know your customer and business. Using the right system, you can easily manage and push the right data to the right place. Lantech retains hundreds of thousands of records on parts and suppliers; we have found that it is easy to program our IT to make certain that suppliers see only the subset that apply to their business with Lantech.

These are examples of how your ERP system, aligned to kanban and lean, can help you rein in and manage the traditional MRP procurement process, free up resources for value-adding activities, and help you collect vital data that is essential for keeping your company competitive. In Chapter 7, we revisit the move from Business Process Kaizen (BPK). The chapter also addresses how dealing with IS obstacles allowed Lantech to "go live" with a new IS system.

CHAPTER 7

Mission to Go Live— Building Teams and Overcoming Barriers

L ANTECH FOCUSED ON MANUFACTURING the first year of our lean transformation. It wasn't long before we could make a machine faster than we could enter the order, so we decided that becoming lean in our business processes was the next logical step. The number one project in Lantech's *hoshin kanri* model for the year (see sidebar below) was implementing a new machine in our product line, which ultimately became the most successful fully lean-developed, designed, manufactured, and sold machine in company history. Management listed Business Process Kaizen (BPK) as the number two project.

Once BPK became a hoshin project, it started the way most of our projects begin, with the assignment of Project Sponsors. The two people assigned were Ron Hicks, who introduced lean to Lantech and has always been our champion, and Jean Cunningham, who functioned in a nonmanufacturing role. Jean and Ron then selected project team members from a wide group of people from different areas of the company, including one person from manufacturing whose role was to help the new team members understand and leverage off Lantech's lean shopfloor successes. Primarily, the people selected for the team were people labeled "overhead." During the year, the overhead team

Setting Your Strategic Intent and Selecting Projects

In Japanese, hoshin means *direction* and *shining needle*; kanri means *management* or *policy* (sometimes referred to as *policy management* or *policy deployment*). Since the early 1960s, hoshin kanri has been an essential tool for lean manufacturing and total quality management, and lately, Six Sigma. From a quality operating system geared to translating the voice of the customer into new products, to a business operating system that ensures reliable growth, to using cross-functional management to integrate the lean supply chain, the yearly hoshin process is about identifying a set of problems or challenges and then designing strategic projects for improvement. The projects then cascade through a network of teams, which include top management, middle management, and ultimately, the entire workforce.

In a lean enterprise, the hoshin kanri process is about empowering those decision makers who add value to a company's products and services so that every level of the company is contributing to delivering customer value. At Lantech, we use it for strategic planning and as a tool for managing projects. Typically, managers from the major departments develop five to seven strategic projects for the year, most often geared to improving processes. Management delegates these projects to project team leaders who assemble teams to implement their particular strategy. The hoshin plan participants vary from year to year, but are primarily top managers and a few selected number twos. Over time, more people get involved, including value stream managers.

During that time, Jean Cunningham and Ron Hicks were an integral part of the hoshin planning team. Everyone involved had opportunity to contribute to strategic plan details; all of the improvement projects had milestone dates and financial goals. The timing of the hoshin plans differed, but they were usually conducted late in the year, prior to the budgeting process. The hoshin plan became an essential part of the organization: We just plain "needed it" to keep pace with the rate of process improvement and project completions.

performed many kaizens in all key areas. People saw that the team was performing valuable work that was integral to the delivery of quality products to our customers, and soon the overhead team became known as the BPK team.

The Business Process Kaizen Team's Strategic Project

This BPK team did not immediately select the kaizen approach to improve Lantech's business processes. Team members read books and interviewed a few consultants with experience in this area. Initially, they had trouble getting a real handle on an improvement approach for business processes, which were so different from the manufacturing processes that readily adapted to lean. Our consultant for manufacturing, TBM, Inc., had not done a great deal of business process consulting, but no one considered this to be an obstacle, and the BPK team was certain that Lantech could apply its lean manufacturing expertise and concepts to the business at hand. The team dived in and, with the support of TBM, began scheduling kaizen events. In the beginning, some skeptical BPK team members could not adjust to the speed of change and the loss of control inherent to kaizen events. They felt that business processes were too complex to have an outside consultant create new ones without preliminary studies by the BPK team. But because kaizen is ultimately about designing, planning, and implementing new processes in the short term, the BPK team could not afford to be slowed down by "anchor draggers." The team was reorganized into a slightly smaller group comprising members excited about promoting the lean approach.

There are many parallels between running a business process kaizen and a manufacturing kaizen. Both, for example, depend on lining up the various support resources for the team. In manufacturing, you will usually need some facilities help to connect electricity or air when you move machines around. Similarly, BPK operated from the

---

Implementation Requires Speed and True Believers

In every company, there are managers and employees that are not interested or willing to engage in change. These are your potential anchor draggers and they tend to be the loudest at the beginning of the change process. Some may eventually "get it" and make adjustments, but there are those who remain stubbornly cynical and even antagonistic to change. Do not waste time convincing these people about the merits of lean. Implementing a lean transformation, or any change in a lean environment requires speed and action. This means training, engaging, and turning early adopters of lean into lean champions, "true believers" who are excited about thinking lean and adept at winning over those who have a wait-and-see attitude. Over time, these champions will help build a common lean culture. For the transition to work, you must let go of those anchor-draggers that you cannot win over. Recognize that they can seriously impede your lean efforts and deflate company morale.

---

assumption that we might need to change locations of people, their computers, and office arrangements, so facilities management was also on our support list. The team also saw the need for information systems and a need to establish guidelines for the way kaizen was utilized. We knew that we would not fix all of the business processes with one kaizen event. As with manufacturing, we would need several kaizen events in many areas. There would be no quick fixes—this was going to take years, not months. With these two underlying premises, the BPK team identified our hydra-headed IS system as a natural target for improvement. This was a no-brainer—everyone knew that the multiple systems making up our IS were horribly inefficient. The team members all had their laundry lists of problems that hindered their performance. When and how to improve our IS was the real question.

The team's first challenge was that we only staffed a small number of IS people with the necessary skills to recode programs. Reprogramming was not an option because it would take too long and detract from the team's goal of tearing down current jobs, making them easier, and creating breakthrough improvements quickly. Rather than be slowed down, the BPK team decided not to make changes to the computer programs, the aim of early kaizen events. Instead, a decision was made to have IS work concurrently with manufacturing. It was also critical for IS people to be active in each kaizen so they knew why the new processes were put in place and so they could later be useful in helping with technology changes. (If dedicating current IS team member time is too difficult or inefficient, drop external training for a year, and put all the "training time" into kaizen events.)

When Lantech's lean shop could no longer improve processes without IS changes, the IS team made changes necessary to support lean improvements. This approach had the added benefit of forcing the kaizen teams to *focus on the process* for overhead functions and redesign them into a smooth effective lean process flow. The teams were required to use the current IS system as they implemented the new improved process. At the same time, they were encouraged to document how they would prefer IS to work with the new process, but no programming changes were allowed. For one year, Ron and Jean, as project sponsors, selected kaizen events in targeted areas while avoiding IS changes. With input from the BPK team, this tactic ultimately flushed out the deficiencies in the current IS program and helped define what we wanted in our new system.

As discussed in Chapter 3, the BPK team identified many wastes and made huge progress in the order entry process; within a two-year time frame, the team was also able to improve customer engineering, materials, and after-sales processes. As the information systems became a barrier to removing waste, the team's improvement pace slowed. At the beginning of year three of our lean journey, Lantech stopped its BPK improvement efforts altogether and began focusing on finding and implementing a new information system (as discussed in Chapter 4).

The BPK Team Becomes the New ERP Team

That year, we made implementing a new ERP one of the five strategic projects on our hoshin model. The ERP implementation change was not about eliminating wastes in the system; it was about removing IS barriers to continued waste elimination for business and manufacturing processes. With this objective in mind, the primary goal was to improve IS response time. Ironically, the only way the BPK team could continue its pace of eliminating wastes was to *stop eliminating business processes waste itself* so it could take the medicine of selecting and implementing a new ERP. It was a necessary evil, prompted by the knowledge that system implementation itself is a big waste—our customers did not care what we were doing behind the scenes to deliver product, and they certainly didn't want to pay for it. When we halted our BPK strategic project and initiated the new system as a strategic project, Jean became the sponsor and leader. The BPK was transformed into a leaner, smaller system team.

In the prior year, the BPK efforts had freed up quite a few people, and the job of the project leader in a lean transformation is to position people with the most varied and flexible skills, people most likely to succeed in leading kaizen follow-up activities, where they are most needed. This means having them work on the next kaizen target or training them for a new job. As discussed in Chapter 4, Lantech's full-time BPK members became the new ERP team, which had five months to select our new ERP system or systems. During this time the IS team prepared the building for a common network and kept the current systems operating.

The new ERP team was highly motivated and enthused. When they finally selected WinMan from TTW, we were all eager to meet the next milestone target—to go live on October 1, 1995. The hoshin model for the strategic project actually had two milestones: The first was to select a product by May 1, and the second was to go live by October 1. For software vendors and for Lantech managers who had been through system implementation at other companies, the target dates were surprising: Some doubted that the deadlines could be met. Despite the time concerns, Jean's confidence was extremely high. She was inspired by three factors:

1. She had observed the impact kaizen events had on changes to the shop floor and business processes over the last two years. Lantech had become accustomed to speed!

2. We had learned that dedicating resources to a top project made the project go three or four times faster than it would with only a part-time commitment.

3. The dedicated team members were the best and the brightest Lantech had to offer because of the company's commitment to using the most talented resources, specifically people whose time had been freed up because of lean initiatives in other areas.

Though this was an unbeatable trilogy, the IS challenge before us was enormous. Our goal was a successful implementation after the first try, and we were determined not to achieve this goal by constantly moving the go live date. The date had been set; the objective was to meet the deadline no matter what. At the same time, we had data everywhere, in multiple systems, multiple product master files, different part numbering systems, multiple customer master files, and even customers with more than one identification number. To top it off, our building did not have proper or adequate wiring for the networks. Delaying the go live date would prolong shutting down our BPK efforts and would siphon some of our top people away from focusing on serving our customers and making better products and solutions. We needed serious help!

Choosing a Consultant and Creating an Implementation Team

Because Lantech had been successful using consultants and kaizen events in its lean journey to eliminate waste, the ERP team wanted a consultant to guide it (not do it) through a successful systems implementation. We wanted someone with real experience, but because the WinMan ERP system was relatively new, finding someone with extensive knowledge of the system would be difficult. We also wanted someone who was able to help us work quickly, someone who could help us achieve all the important target dates. In most lean projects, a company has some time and variability for implementation and can use pilot runs, such as in manufacturing, or even implement in stages. Occasionally, there may even be time to review and redo the effort to make it run more smoothly. This is not so in an ERP implementation because "trial and error" when implementing a new system is an unaffordable luxury. The cost of the ERP implementation in time, dollars, and morale of "doing it again to get it right" is simply too high.

As luck would have it, however, we found a consultant, Gene Caiola, whose specialty was working with companies to salvage an ERP implementation that had gone awry. Choosing Gene Caiola meant we had someone who knew all the serious pitfalls to avoid in implementing a new ERP. Because of this, we felt like we were always one step ahead of the implementation process. We learned that while the team had to do the work, they were the ones who knew lean, and what lean meant at Lantech, we were not afraid to get help to guarantee success. Rework and redundant efforts are some of the seven deadly wastes, and we didn't want to risk introducing them into our project.

The new ERP team set a go live target of October 1, and Gene joined our effort in June. It was agreed that TTW would come on site on July 1 to begin to implement WinMan. At this point, it was time to form an implementation team, which consisted of six people: three from the new ERP team and three new people. Table 7-1 shows the new team's areas of focus. As the table illustrates, four of the team members were dedicated to full-time work on the implementation. *They had no other duties. Implementation to the schedule date was the 100 percent focus.* The implementation team also got a new name: the Wizard Team (see sidebar.)

Table 7-1. The Implementation Team Becomes the Wizard Team

	Lantech's Wizard Team	
Team Member	Role	Commitment
Jean Cunningham	Project Manager facilitating the overall implementation process. Arranged resources, set meetings, and generally resolved team barriers.	50%
Rick Norris	Equipment Sales Processes. Specifically worked on the order entry process.	100%
Duane Jones	Engineering Procurement, Inventory, Manufacturing. Duane worked on the customer engineering and manufacturing processes.	100%
Cathy Taylor	Accounting	50%
Debbie Thompson	After-Market Sales and Service	100%
Jeanne Belanger	Overarching Process consultant and support, and later, a floater where help was needed.	100%

There were eventually other additions to the Wizard Team, not always by design but always welcome. Various associates from TTW, Joe and Scott Wilkinson, Nick Jacobs, and Jonathan Cranford, quickly became players in a strong partnership. They gave the same or greater fervor to the project as other members of the team, and it became a powerful combination of resources. Today, we continue to enjoy their presences, as friends and as colleagues.

The Wizard

Jeanne Belanger became a floater by fate, not by design. Before our IS journey, Jeanne had been one of our top manufacturing managers on the floor. During our BPK process, however, we discovered some artificial organizational structures that did not make sense. When we looked for someone to make sense of these structures, we found Jeanne, a creative, versatile, and gutsy leader with the confidence to call Bill Gates's people to tell them about our company and what we could offer them. Jeanne was never afraid of a challenge. She also had a sterling quality that is the hallmark of a good leader: Everyone who worked for her respected her because she respected her people.

Jeanne was chosen to head up the effort to find our ERP and did much of the preliminary work in sorting through what was available in the marketplace. During the implementation of WinMan, she worked whenever she could and was fully committed to the project.

When fate dealt Jeanne a cruel hand, cancer, the entire team was grief-stricken. Well loved and admired, she had done much to make our work fluid and sensible. In tribute to this amazing woman, we decided to name our new ERP after her: Jeanne was our Genie, and the ERP became Wizard, a magical approach that would put all the information we needed at the tip of the IS wand and at the tip of the fingers that would be using it.

Managing the Implementation

In his role as advisor, Gene Caiola visited our plant for two days. He spent the first day talking with each team member and the TTW associates on site, reviewing progress and barriers. This gave him a good feel for where we were moving rapidly, where we were stalling, and about unexpected events occurring along the way. The second day he was at the plant he facilitated a meeting with the entire Wizard Team. We set the targets for completion for the next six weeks, taking into consideration the progress and barriers of the prior six weeks. Everything was organized with the go live date of October 1, giving the project a sense of urgency and augmenting the already high level of motivation among team members bound by a singular compelling goal. During these meetings, we made trade-offs and choices. For example, we emphasized some reports and de-emphasized others, which did not seem as important to design and complete. Some were put on hold indefinitely. At the other extreme were certain "sacred" capabilities that were not part of any trade-off discussions. This included kanban, actual cost accounting, and manufacturing visually without work orders. A clear strategic intent that was backed by the company, along with a strongly facilitated plan of attack and full-time dedicated resources, saved the Wizard Team from ever having to pick and choose among core ERP capabilities. We got everything we wanted.

One important decision was to design the Wizard meeting room for the maximum output for capturing and sharing information. We used a huge whiteboard that showed the macro plan and the six-week plan so that everyone on the team could see where we were. A key element was the room arrangement: desks for each team member in a U-shaped cell (just like in manufacturing) with no cubicle or physical walls separating people. Each team member had immediate access to other team members to talk about issues, make decisions, or review interesting ERP functions on the computer. No time was wasted on setting up meetings or scheduling information-sharing sessions: The team spent nearly 100 percent of its time on activities directed at going live, and the meetings and information sharing session occurred naturally and spontaneously at a central site that was conducive to communication and equipped with immediate visual updates: the whiteboard and the many flip charts hanging on the walls, showing the work in process. Additionally, the team encouraged other company people to drop in and look over the plans, and these invitations were eagerly accepted.

One of the major activities that team members engaged in was preparing and testing modules within their respective areas. Each member followed more or less the same eight-step process:

1. *Getting data ready.* This included preparing the customer master file, part master file, supplier master files, employee master files, and chart of accounts. This step was a major task because the company IS used multiple systems to store data in many areas. There were no shortcuts, just the hard work of plowing through the information, looking for redundancies, and resolving them. The number one focus for each team member was filling in the core information for each data field that was critical for going live.

2. *Testing the modules.* We used the lean approach of thoroughly testing before moving to the next stage or implementing. On the shop floor, a lean manufacturer checks quality at the source rather than at the end of the line. The team member made certain that each module worked properly with the data before testing the whole system.

3. *Making recommended changes to the modules.* Team members tested each module and functionality, documenting any needed modifications, and giving this feedback to the TTW associate on site at the time. TTW worked to the same priority as the ERP team.

4. *Testing the changes to the modules.* Team members would sign off on the changes and prepare the next step.

5. *Writing operating procedures for each person who would use the information system in that particular process.* The test transactions were helpful. The team members picked a wide

variety of orders that represented an array of situations: parts orders, distributor orders, complex equipment, simple equipment, multiple line items, orders with deposits, etc.

6. *Creating a test packet of transactions that were used to test the system.* The team ran the information gathered in steps five and six through the modules to see how the system handled the information.

7. *Preparing the system test.* Once the team had tested all the modules, the reference data were prepared, and all the system indicators were set up, we ran a system test, starting with the business process flow as an order would normally run.

8. *Setting up the reference data (dates, holidays, part status codes).* Each Wizard Team member had a special focus. Even though we moved forward with common goals, each area had unique or special setups. For instance, the calendar for manufacturing was a four-day work week, while in after-market it was 24/7.

You would think that after testing all the modules, the system test would be easy, but there were some flaws and glitches. However, each process owner knew the area so thoroughly that he or she was able to spot these quickly and immediately resolve them.

Going Live—Strike for the Heart

Probably every implementation team has had debates on whether to go live in parallel or to just jump off the bridge and go live with no back up. This is an important question even if you are implementing only one module. Implementing *every* module in *every* part of the company makes this an extremely complex issue. People outside our Wizard Team wanted us to be careful, and urged us to have a backup, to go in parallel, and so on. These are some of the same concerns people have on the shop floor before fully understanding what it means to have *breakthrough* kaizen events. The Wizard Team members saw the commitment on the shop floor and knew they could spend days and weeks training and preparing the workers. They also knew we could continue both systems for only a very short period. At the same time, from a practical perspective, the Wizard Team felt that training people in advance was not a good idea. Trained too soon, they would likely forget most of what they learned. In addition, our workforce was pretty lean, with most of the employees spending time on value add or other necessary activities. It would be hard to run two systems at the same time. Finally, we did not want to launch the new system with expectations of failure. Most successful lean companies using kaizen events don't hesitate to implement changes; they strike for the heart. With all of these considerations in mind, we decided to burn our IS bridge to the past and create a new bridge to a leaner future. This approach immediately sent a message throughout the company that there was no going back: The new ERP *must* work and the workforce *must* help it to work.

Even the best implementation schemes cannot change everything "perfectly" at the same time, so we factored in some preparation time. In every area, Wizard Team members held training sessions a few days leading up to the go live date. In connection with this, they put up big flip charts, called barrier boards, in each area. Just like in manufacturing, when a problem arises in building an order, the first line of resolution is a consultation with the team leader. If it is not resolved, the line support member writes up the problem on the barrier board for later resolution. We used the same type of approach with the system implementation. The Wizard Team leader stayed in the area where the work was being done. When someone had a problem using the system, he or she raised a white flag. The Wizard member would go to that person and resolve the issue (always showing and teaching, not doing). If the person could not resolve the problem, the Wizard member wrote the problem on the barrier board for the rest of the team to see and respond to. If a new learning tool or idea was identified, this too would go up on the board. We did experience a few showstopper problems: flaws that had to be fixed to proceed. When this occurred, TTW associates (already on site) would assist our ERP team with the fix.

The Challenge of Using Fewer Reports

Not everything went well with the new system implementation. In the old system, employees looked up data, sent transactions to the system, and created new reports to determine what to do next. Basically, users were accustomed to working with reports. In contrast, an ERP system is not very report driven. It is more interactive. You click your way through orders, receive parts, backflush inventory, create invoices, receive payment, and pay bills. Because people were unaccustomed to the new system, the Wizard Team received many requests for reports.

Distance Is Not a Factor

TTW's home office is in England. When we began evaluating the ERP products, we thought having a partner in a distant time zone was a big minus. Much to our amusement, we later learned that some people at TTW initially thought we were more interested in a trip to England than in their product. How totally wrong we both turned out to be! As we began the implementation process, TTW programmers came to Louisville for two-week intervals at a time. They worked really long days . . . good bang for the buck! They did all the programming (the Wizard and IS teams did not program). If we had a problem that the home office needed to resolve, we would tell them about it by e-mail, usually near the end of our day, when they were still asleep. By the time the Wizard team arrived for work the following day, we usually had an answer. The bottom line here is that you should not let a few miles (or even a few thousand miles) keep you from a good vendor.

Because the Wizard Team members understood the business, however, they could easily determine which reports were critical, not so critical, and no longer necessary. The real trick was to pass this knowledge on to people who were becoming adjusted to the new system and decrease the number of report requests. One way the Wizard Team made this happen was to place all report requests on a list with a priority rank that was available to all system users, allowing people to see for themselves how long it might be until a particular request was addressed. The list was a wonderful control mechanism. At first, the Wizard Team met daily to address the list. As the implementation process progressed, the number of report request meetings dwindled. As the employees became more familiar with the new system, their report needs dissipated, and it became unnecessary to address most of the original report requests. Few new requests appeared.

Importance of Teams in Building a Lean Culture

Throughout the book, the authors have stressed how Lantech uses its best people for its various cross-functional teams and kaizens. However, team building is also about having clear objectives and strategies, such as hoshin projects, that empower the team to make tough decisions. Team building is about using common tools to develop a common language, and giving team members time to learn to work closely together, sometimes in the same room, for months or years. We used teams to establish lean in our manufacturing; developing teams in our BPK effort was another logical progression at creating a lean culture throughout the company.

Like continuous improvement, team building is an ongoing daily effort. Having a team does not mean all decisions are consensus-based. But it does mean that all team members are aware of decisions and have an opportunity to contribute as needed or desired. There should be no secrets or sacred cows in a team's area of responsibility.

Choosing the right team members and developing a group that works well together is extremely important, especially when implementing a targeted go live date. In the case of implementing ERP, having team members with various business process backgrounds helped build the cohesiveness necessary to work directly with IS, TTW, and our consultant, Gene.

At this point, some thought should also be given to what happens after a team process is finished. Generally, it resurfaces in a different form. After four months of intense focus on going live, running tests, changing modules, and training employees, the day finally came when the Wizard Team eventually disbanded, its mission completed. We had a big celebration and then went our separate ways. Duane migrated to Information Systems. He learned to program, and is now our information communication technology team leader. Rick, who had responsibility for orders, became a regional sales manager and remained available for information systems for sales needs. Debbie, who had responsibility for after-market processes, became our after-market parts business team leader, taking responsibility for over 10 percent of our business revenues. Cathy is one of our accounting team leaders, and can find information in the system like no one else. Our good friend Jeanne was with us until January 1996. We were all sad to see her go, and the Wizard Team members never look at the Wizard symbol without thinking of her.

CHAPTER 8

Capturing, Managing, and Sharing Information

Whether you are a general planning a battle, a student preparing for exams, or a corporate executive who is thinking of implementing a new system or process, the more information you have, the better equipped you are to make good decisions and take appropriate action. Certainly, too much information can slow you down, particularly if there is a wide range of analytical tools to choose from or if you have an inherent propensity for overanalyzing. Both factors may lead to (or exacerbate) indecision. On the other hand, too little knowledge is indeed a dangerous thing, so it is probably better to err on the side of caution and have more information than you need rather than less. Generally speaking, most of the people making decisions in your organization would probably agree with the latter view.

Information is what an ERP system captures and manages, and this should be a primary consideration when deciding to implement ERP. In the course of performing the multitude of tasks that run your business, your ERP system will capture and store millions of pieces of information that become increasingly more valuable as your company seeks new and better ways to serve your customer.

Who Sees the Information?

One of the most important decisions you must make about the information your ERP collects is who should see it. In a lean company, it is essential for everyone who does the work to have access to the information they need. This certainly doesn't mean that everybody sees everything. There may be a few areas, such as HR for instance, that should have limited access. Lantech's WinMan ERP system is limited only to information relevant to running the business. If people poke around the system for the fun of it, there is no danger that they will access data they should not be seeing. In most cases, employees poke around when a system is new, usually just to explore its capabilities. Once the system becomes a familiar fixture, they generally tend to focus on options and information they need to perform their respective jobs. In transforming your information systems for a lean environment, follow IS guiding principle #3, *the primary purpose of security is to avoid data corruption and provide information access.* IS enables

---

Ask and You Should Receive

One of our material handlers, Gary Young, asked for information to assist in organizing his area. He needed to know how often we sold certain types of options. In a more traditional company, that information might be maintained or controlled by a sales or marketing group. In a lean company, you put the information in front of the person who needs it. Gary was given access to reporting tools providing a full breakdown of models and options, and pricing and cost for order entry and shipments. It was more information than he needed, but we trusted he would use what he needed and not worry about the rest. A side benefit is that Gary is very familiar with his area. Giving him a broader view of the work allows him to see additional opportunities for improvement.

---

your employees to provide value-add and serve your customers. Accessible and accurate information drives your business and provides the real data needed to identify future initiatives, which may end up as a project in your hoshin planning.

Lantech has a companywide practice allowing all of its employees to access all business-related information across departments. This practice is especially important for kaizen events. Moreover, if an associate has time for extra work outside of his or her normal field, IS can point this person in the right direction to access the required program.

Within this structure, security (i.e., Can the people who access this information be trusted?) is not a big concern. Neither is the initial problem with incorrect interpretation. As with most innovations introduced into a business, you will find there is a learning curve. As people learn the system and its capabilities, they will fine-tune their skills and get better at using it. Just give them the access they need. Up and down the organization, access to ERP breaks down potential barriers that often hinder quick decisions and communication across functions and teams, and interfere with the speed you need in your kaizen events.

Benefits of Open Sharing of Information

Open sharing helps team members and management know what people are doing. For example, during the course of normal daily operations, a user may contact IS to gain access to a program. Perhaps this user has seen a program someone else is using or is involved in a new project and believes the program will help. You may want to know why this person wants access, because knowing what new process a person is engaged in is always informative, but your most important role in this process is to steer the person in the right direction.

Open sharing of information also saves time. If a user needs information from another area, waiting for someone else to provide it is wasteful; so is interrupting someone else engaged in other tasks. Waiting impedes the one-piece flow of information. With direct access, users can perform their tasks seamlessly. Being interrupted to dole out bits of information disrupts work in process. To eliminate this problem, we have IS provide a space in the system or a link to a page where people can post and update their information so that it is readily available to others. Because the information is easily accessible, chronic interruption is no longer an issue. Our kaizen teams also identify waiting wastes (bottlenecks) in the system and works with IS to eliminate these.

Example of Easy Access—Programming a Preorder Screen

Lantech's effort to improve its preorder process was discussed in Chapter 3, but we revisit it here in connection with the theme of easy access. We measure our sales performance on a monthly basis, and at the end of each month, there is usually a bit of scurrying about to see what orders are available and can be added into the current month. In some ways, this may be a company character flaw, but it is what it is. Prior to 1998, at month's end, the various sales managers were calling or receiving calls from salesmen, quoters, and order entry associates, trying to track down the status of new orders. It was never certain who the owner was for each piece of information. As a result, three different people could end up calling the same person asking the same question or calling numerous other people until they found out who had what they wanted.

IS created a Preorder Screen function in our ERP (see Figure 8-1). It began with basic information. When a sales order arrived by fax or e-mail, the order was added to the Preorder Screen. We recorded the customer name, the type of product ordered, the customer purchase order number, and the salesperson in charge. This eliminated a lot of phone calls because everyone could now look in one place to see what orders were pending. However, salespeople were still asking for additional information, and IS added approximate sales dollars, a series of checkboxes to indicate the barrier to closing the order, and a general notes section. Now the screen contains enough information to answer most questions and eliminates the waste of providing redundant

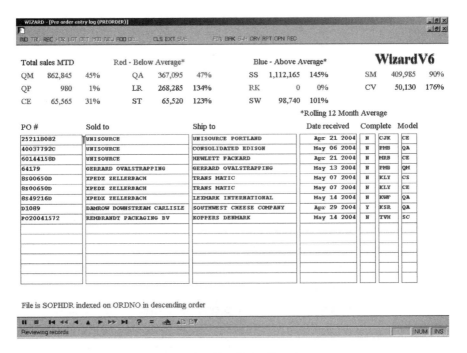

Figure 8-1. Pre-Order Entry Log

Four Simple Examples of the Benefits of Sharing Data

1. *Accounts Receivable needs service data.* The job of accounts receivable is to collect the money owed the company as quickly as possible. However, there is nothing more annoying to a customer than getting a collection call when the machine recently purchased has problems or you delivered it late. While this happens rarely, it does happen, and data sharing becomes part of the damage control. Sometimes, it can prevent the damage from occurring at all. Have your field service team share information about any machine problems so your accounts receivable people can see data on delivery and quickly tailor their collection approach to any special situations.

(continued on next page)

(continued from previous page)

2. *Purchasing needs to see new R&D developments.* As you make longer commitments with the supply chain partners, it is critical that purchasing buyers see information from the Research and Development teams on what types of part changes might be released. With this information in hand, they can minimize the purchase volumes on those parts.

3. *Shipping area needs data to clear shipments.* A kaizen in the shipping area identified waste generated by shipping associates who were regularly contacting accounting to confirm machines had been cleared for shipment. They would stop work to make such calls and sometimes waited to hear back before proceeding. To combat this waste, we added a place in the ERP for accounting to identify proactively which machines were cleared for shipment. A further improvement was to poka-yoke the shipment process, blocking machines that had not been cleared. A later follow-up was automatic notification when a machine was near shipment but not yet cleared by accounting.

4. *HR needs data to manage resources.* Even HR may use order volume data to anticipate the company's needs for additional permanent or temporary staff, or the need to transfer resources within the organization. Providing the means for HR or management to identify the company's capacity needs and plan accordingly, can avoid many potential bottleneck headaches.

As information sharing becomes routine within the company, the possibilities for using it to improve productivity become endless. It plays an essential role in continuous improvement.

information. The order entry team has to log in the order information only once, and anyone can review the pending orders and see what issues may exist. With the new system in place, we now avoid dealing with the repetitive and inefficient way information was being moved about from person to person.

Open Information Builds Trust and a Common Culture

A less tangible benefit to sharing information is that it fosters consistency in how people correct and update information. When a specific part of the business holds or controls information, the controlling group may develop a tendency to massage the information before releasing it. In extreme cases, people may start correcting or hiding errors, falsifying and corrupting information that will be used somewhere else. If you share information in real time, you lose control over it. Skewed data are easier to detect, and knowing that information is available in real time companywide is a pretty good deterrent to this practice. In an open system, there is no place to hide. Information is in plain sight.

The true benefit, however, is that your employees learn to load and retrieve information right the first time; they also accept responsibility for the work, acknowledge errors, and learn to work with others to correct them. This improves productivity and teaches employees to be more flexible. Having common access to immediate information changes your "closed" culture, creating more trust and interdependency. It is a cornerstone of good team building.

Building an open culture is not easy, but using your ERP to share information can make it easier. In a company environment, everyone in the order fulfillment process contributes information. The individual contributing the information may never use it again, or see any personal benefit in keeping it. But the combined collection and distribution of open information empowers other employees and the company as a whole in serving the customer. In other words, it contributes to the greater whole and supports common goals that are part of the common culture.

Sharing information requires some self-sacrifice. The personal return is uncertain and employees may not see its immediate value.

But training your employees to understand their role in using ERP to capture and share information about the company's business and customers will go a long way in helping them understand their role in a lean culture. It builds trust throughout the company. And trust is a valuable commodity with kaizen events and leadership. In essence, this is a classic example of IS principle #12, *Productivity for all is more important than productivity for one.*

Lantech has always been open to sharing financial information. After the end of each month, we have a companywide meeting during which co-owner and CEO Jim Lancaster shares order entry and shipment dollar numbers with the group and explains how those numbers will impact profit sharing for the quarter. It takes time for some new associates to trust that this information is accurate and shared for the benefit of all, especially if their experiences in other corporate environments have taught them to mistrust management and management's numbers. Once they use the ERP system, however, they change their minds. The first thing everyone sees when they log on to the system is a posting of shipment and order entry dollars for the month and year to date. In fact, anyone who logs on to the system on the first day of the month knows the final numbers before Jim does. If an employee is still skeptical, he or she can verify the numbers by taking a calculator and adding up all the sales orders.

Trust between management and workers is extremely valuable. You can't buy it or sell it, but it definitely pays dividends. It builds loyalty and morale, and it improves productivity. Instilling such trust requires a conscious effort by company leadership, and one of the best ways to do this is to open up information and train your employees to use it well.

Use Information as a Tool Throughout Your Business

Some of the tangible benefits we have discovered from collecting and using data revolve around IS guiding principle #13, *Huge data stores are easy to manipulate.* Lantech has collected a massive amount of information about its customers and the company's relationship with them. Some of our salespeople have become masters at taking that information and demonstrating to our customers not just the total cost of ownership of our product but also the *total value of their relationship with Lantech*. We provide high-quality equipment and top-quality service, and we have the data to make that a selling point to our customers.

Similarly, Lantech has collected an incredible amount of data regarding its relationship with distribution partners. We know and document the value they provide, and we also know and document the value we provide. Knowing the history and details of both ends of a relationship drives you to improve that relationship, which further increases its value. We have the facts and data to tell us where to focus our efforts to help both Lantech and our partners deliver and continuously improve. In a lean world, there is no better way to show your appreciation for a good relationship.

Our company has exhaustive data that help us identify the value of our supply chain partners. We can easily identify the parts, quantities, and dollars for each supplier. We can see quality and delivery problems, and we can see excellence as well as improvements. We use this information to increase or decrease business or to negotiate improved pricing.

As your company grows leaner, you will learn to share and use information as a useful tool for all your business processes. This tool will help you measure what is already there, identify opportunities for proactive change, and implement improvements across the board.

The New IS Role in Supporting Lean

By design, the IS department played a marginal role in Lantech's IS transformation. During manufacturing kaizens, we eliminated standard cost accounting and adopted a single methodology for part numbers. At the same time, we adjusted the manufacturing system. As previously noted, when we began our business processes kaizen efforts, we purposely did NOT make many IS changes because the BPK team wanted to get the processes right before doing the necessary IS programming. One reason we made very few changes in our information systems is that there was no clear path to making IS lean. As discussed in the introduction to this book, there is probably no distinct IS value stream, although IS touches and influences many points in your main value streams: 1) *problem solving,* 2) *information management,* and 3) *physical transformation (manufacturing flow).* The easiest way to comprehend this is to view IS as one of the processes within your other value streams. To use this process effectively, your company must first identify and eliminate wastes in these other value streams, improve their processes as much as possible, and then determine how best *to align IS to continue the lean process.* The key learning point here is that the IS transformation works best if you make IS programming changes *after* process improvements.

This book opened with an anecdotal conversation between an information systems manager and a CEO. When the CEO informed the information systems manager that the company had decided to go lean and manufacturing needed IS to help in every way it could, the IS manager's big question was "What now?" The two critical concerns for the IS manager were how to partner (not get in the way) with the lean efforts, and how to eliminate wastes and apply lean principles in IS operations. Table 1-1 identified some common wastes and clearly laid out how manufacturing and business kaizen teams should drive the process, including choosing the new IS system. The IS role for selecting and implementing a new information system is straightforward— the IS team needs to facilitate the kaizen teams as well as understand the deliverables for lean thinking. Previous chapters in this book provide many examples of where and how IS teams can lend their support in this way. Thus, the second concern—how to eliminate wastes and apply lean principles in IS operations—is really about the new role of

IS *after* lean processes are in place. This basically means looking at what has changed, what is the same, and how IS can continue to be a lean partner in a lean environment in a lean way.

When the IS team no longer is a slave to a list of system enhancement requests haphazardly thrown at programmers, but is proactively reaching out and partnering with the value streams, team members will know they have developed flow and will make proactive contributions in the lean organization. The IS team supports flow by keeping the backlog of requests low and by working closely with users to develop the right enhancements the first time. Instead of being the tail on the dog, your information system will become a vital part of the hunt for customer value.

Of course, all of this depends on how IS captures and manages information. Dealing directly with this is guiding principle #9, *Archive customer history; 'clean house' on internal transactions.* Not all data is created equal, so the IS team needs to know which data to keep long term and which data to dump. It is very important to perform housecleaning chores and to organize the data so anyone can easily access it. The intent is to keep customer information available at all times and keep short-term internal information out of the way but accessible if needed. IS should have clear instructions about this and have complete faith in guiding principle #13, *Huge data stores are easy to manipulate.* With this guideline in mind, IS can effectively store customer information, such as customer orders, while simultaneously archiving information that has short-term value, such as inventory transactions and internal scheduling. Both tasks are part of an integrated system, and neither intrudes upon or impedes the other.

Another ongoing IS task after improving your processes is adherence to guiding IS principle #8, *Capture everything you can about your customer.* The IS team needs to 1) *know who the customer is,* 2) *set up nonstructured formats to capture customer information,* 3) *create an organized method for saving the data,* and 4) *help train people to access and store the data.* To accomplish this, IS needs to keep its options broad. The idea is to continuously look for and/or suggest the best possible solution to the company's need for information. Technology in this area is always changing, and IS should be a leading force in training the workforce on new methodologies.

Traditionally, providing security has been purely an IS function directed at guarding against outside intruders as well as at providing internal guidelines for managing employee access. However, it bears repeating, both the company and IS need to change the mind-set on this issue and view security as a means to support the lean environment by openly sharing information. The focus should be on IS guiding principle #3, *Primary purpose of security is to avoid data corruption and provide information access.* Of course, protection from worms and viruses and updating software and security are still the province of IS, but this must be balanced with providing easy and safe access for employees. Without jeopardizing security, IS must remove restrictions to accessing information when such restrictions cause employees to wait for needed information. This is pure waste. By programming your information system to capture and deliver information seamlessly your IS team contributes directly to delivering on the lean principle of flow, *eliminating the non-value adding activities in the value stream so that a product's progression flows unimpeded continuously.*

The point that has been continuously underscored throughout this book is that you need to develop an information system that supports your lean changes and captures vital information in all value streams, in real time, shared and leveraged by all. The true value add of IS is that it helps to bind the entire company to this end. Achieve this, and you will not only cut waste and improve costs, you will find yourself in a good place: a vantage point that allows you to see what really matters to your customers and the value you must deliver to serve them—the first principle of lean thinking.

CHAPTER 9

Lean Accounting Systems

I N TRADITIONAL COMPANIES, much of what comprises information systems deals with accounting, and almost all traditional information systems include focus on standard cost accounting. You could write a whole book on the accounting changes you need to make as a lean manufacturer, and, in fact, such a book already exists: *Real Numbers, Management Accounting for a Lean Organization*, by Jean Cunningham and Orest Fiume. The book you are currently reading, however, focuses specifically on what you need to know (based on the changes you want to make in accounting) about the changes you need to make in your information systems.

In some ways, information systems and accounting are strange bedfellows. In the area of IS, the technology changes so rapidly, that IT language and tools may be obsolete within 18 months. Change is a given and IS managers are constantly adjusting themselves to accommodate this. Accounting, on the other hand, is a rather conservative discipline, and there is a tendency to resist changes in thinking or methodology. Nevertheless, IS and accounting are inexorably tied to each other by a unique similarity: Neither IS nor accounting has much to do with the process of doing business (i.e., delivering the product or service), yet both are essential for providing companies with the information needed to conduct business.

This chapter will describe the changes needed to support or enable the somewhat radical changes in thinking that your accountants will need to make as you move into the lean environment. We have already addressed some of these topics, order entry and kanban, in the other chapters. This chapter introduces two related topics: Plain English Financial Statements and Elimination of Standard Cost Accounting. Other changes may arise as accountants embrace lean and find additional creative ways to simplify and eliminate waste in their work.

The Role of Reports in Lean

As your kaizen teams look for waste, one area they will explore is how your company uses reports. In the process, you will virtually eliminate your paper reports, and those that remain will be very different from the traditional reports your company once generated. Training report writers to deal with this change will become very important. Rather than trying to teach everyone to write reports, you will first need to identify the person(s) in each area who has an interest in IT because it is a lot easier to teach someone that is interested than someone who is just "supposed" to learn. Focus on training at least one user in each area. Once these people become adept at writing the kind of reports you will need, they will become your "super users," people with a deep understanding of how the data in their respective processes are organized and the ability to see the potential of new applications or techniques to eliminate waste.

The canned reports in most information systems are a fairly good starting point. Be aware, however, that most of these reports are written by programmers who know and are concerned with database management rather than with the business purposes of the reports (e.g., ordering parts, looking for discrepancies, or collecting money). You must also be aware that while it would be nice to eliminate paper reports altogether, this is not likely to happen. What will happen is that the reports will be tailored to function as support tools for lean thinking. The example below demonstrates this concept.

Among standard accounting reports generated by traditional IT systems, is one that shows the amount of money owed by each customer and how long it is overdue, usually called the Accounts Receivable Aging Report. Canned reports generally organize this information by customer number. A far better way to use IT is to tailor the report to a specific function, in this case collections. The sequence of the IT canned report was not in Customer Name order but in Customer Number order. By observing the collections function, it becomes obvious that the aging report is really a preplanning report and that the most useful data for such a report to show is correlations. To eliminate waste of searching for related accounts, you need a report that is organized alphabetically by customer name. This format works well for a number of reasons. Some customers, for example, have more than one account. Seeing the accounts side by side, the collection analyst can look at the total account status when prepping for a collection call. The format can also make it easier to detect posting errors, thus signaling that some collection calls are not necessary.

Another good modification to consider for this kind of IT report is rearranging or adjusting column headings to reflect real-time needs. Most aging reports have the following columns: Current, < 30 days past due, 30–60 days past due, 60–90 days past due, > 90 days. When we used this traditional structure at Lantech, the kaizen team found that the main reason for customers not paying their bills on time was because they did not know they owed money. In addition, many customers who had a bill due on the 30th day of a billing cycle put the payment in the mail on the 30th day. When the payment arrived, it was applied in the 35–40 day range. The collections analyst would usually assume that everything in the < 30 days past due column was in transit, and the company waited for payment to arrive. This, after all, was "normal" and was supported by the column arrangement of the report. It did not take long to realize that waiting a full 30 days beyond the due date seemed wasteful. What was needed was a simple adjustment to the report. We added a < 15 days late column and a 15–30 days late column, which changed "normal" to mean that payment delays created by the report itself would no longer be sanctioned. Now the analyst can skip the < 15 days column, but jump right on the 15–30 days items, quickly identifying what should be billed and when to drop outstanding receivables and improve the company's cash level.

The example above is not to propose that this is the type of change needed in your company, but to show that information systems are flexible, that canned reports can be easily modified, and that small changes can yield very big dividends.

Standard Cost Accounting

As the book *Real Numbers* notes, "In a traditional manufacturing environment, an attempt is made at cost control using standard cost and variance analysis. Many companies have armies of cost accountants poring over variance reports after month end, trying to determine their reason for variances. The problem is . . . it is virtually impossible to trace an unfavorable variance to its root cause." Also compounding this problem in the lean organization is the rate of rapid change on the shop floor in how you manufacture the product. The authors of *Real Numbers* further observe, "The role of cost control in a lean environment is to reduce cost by eliminating waste. . . . Look at profitability in terms of groups of products."

In connection with this, your lean company will most likely begin to reassess the cost basis of your products, which will probably include eliminating standard cost accounting for some or all of your products. But what does it mean to your information systems? Because you have dramatically changed the processing of products and dramatically reduced the work in process (WIP), you will no longer get any benefit from standard cost absorption. The absorption part of eliminating standard cost accounting has to do with the labor accounting and the overhead accounting, the greatest waste generator of nonuseful information in a lean cellular manufacturing company. The good news is that you will probably not have to do much programming (even to your 'vanilla' system) to implement this change. In Appendix I, we provide a step-by-step approach to shutting down the standard cost system. It takes three basic steps to make this change:

- Step 1: Ensure that there are no reconciling items between your accounting system and your inventory system.

- Step 2: Use the features included when you do a cost roll. (Cost roll is the function used when you are changing the standard cost for your full product lines. It may have a different name in your system, but every manufacturing module will have one.) In this case, the change is the same, except that instead of changing the labor or overhead rates to a new amount, you will change them to Zero! Presto! You have used the existing functionality for an entirely different purpose. The only trouble spot may be software that has one of those pesky, mistake-proofing features that will not allow you to set the value to zero. Hopefully, a good system setup will let you override that "friendly" but annoying feature.

- Step 3: Deal with the material components on the BOM of your products. You can make a decision to have standard cost (and all the derivatives) or actual cost. You can make this decision independently of your decision to eliminate absorption accounting. Again, use the standard functionality of the software, making the same decision you would have to when originally setting up the software. Good results will come from using the basic features of the software. If you switch from one method to another, there may be some lag time for the newly cosseted items to flow through, but your accountants should easily understand this.

When you do eliminate standard cost accounting, it does not mean you will never have or use it in your ERP system again. It just means that every transaction on the shop floor will not generate the labor reporting of variance, overhead variance, adjustments to inventory, and the confusion that typically plagues those people using this information. Your company will still probably need a place where it can store benchmark information for a product, maybe even to the part level. That information can be very helpful for analysis, pricing, and other trend reporting. It will, however, not be driving regular profit reporting.

Plain English Financial Statement

With the absorption gone, you may get a request to create a much greater number of financial reporting structures than you had before the changeover. *Real Numbers* refers to these simple types of income statements as *Plain English Financial Statements*. They have this moniker because the elements of cost use the plain English terms like payroll cost, rent, and utilities rather than their business jargon equivalents of standard cost, variance, or mix. Plain English Financial Statements are easy to produce, even on a daily basis, and easy for users to understand. In fact, the accountants will probably want a quick tool to create such financial statements on demand for all departments, for groups of departments, or even for an individual department. An Excel macro can be most helpful in reporting these different slices of the business in a consistent manner. You will probably use and delete these slices of reporting at individual desktops; there is no need to store them long term.

Putting Financial Statements in the Hands of the Users

If your software is capable of creating multiple income statements based on different "cuts" of the information, you are in luck. (You may need both separated income statements and balance sheets. Or you may need one balance sheet for a group of products.) If your software does not have this capability, you may want to export your information to macros, using spreadsheet software like Excel.

Lantech had quite a philosophical debate on this issue. One side claimed that exporting data to Excel from the general ledger system meant losing the control to ensure the data are not changed. The other side argued that moving to Excel would make it easy to manipulate data to create the most useful format for the business. The argument that tipped the scales and made us decide to export to Excel was that we could, at any time, generate a macro financial statement from the system (standard format) and compare it with the same level income statement in Excel to ensure the results were consistent.

The biggest winners were the users. With the new financial statement format and with Excel, a tool most were familiar with, they could produce analysis and comparisons far beyond what is possible with a static report. All users were given access; all were also given the means to locate and use the financial reports stored in Excel network documents.

Impact of Kanban on Accounts Payable Functions

Chapter 5 deals with many of the issues of that affect purchasing when using kanban methodology. By the same token, no discussion of system changes in the accounting area would be complete without a discussion of the impact of kanban on the accounts payable functions. One of the most dramatic aspects of this is that kanban increases the number of materials receipts because products are delivered more frequently.

The first reaction has to be anxiety about an inbox that is suddenly flooded with invoices, maybe four or five times the normal amount. The second reaction is wondering, "How did that happen?" It happened because of kanban. After implementing kanban with your suppliers, you will potentially receive a shipment from every vendor on a daily basis (or even more frequently), and nearly every company sends out an invoice to the customer for every shipment! This was not a problem in the more traditional approach, which normally meant purchasing in larger batches on the premise that bulk purchasing translated to bulk pricing and savings on shipping costs. In addition, buying in bulk meant fewer and less frequent vendor shipments: weekly or once a month. The tradeoff is easy to see: With lean thinking there are more invoices, but this is offset by awesome savings in space, managing inventory, improved quality, better cash management, and a surprising lack of price increases for the smaller, more frequent shipments you receive by using kanban purchasing.

Woe to the accounts payable team that has not kept pace with the company's lean improvements. Such a team's first line of defense at being caught off guard might be to demand that IS speed up the system so team members can process more invoices. But this is firefighting at its worst. Lean thinking's answer is to take the bull (or in this case, the vendors) by the horns and tell them to stop invoices. Although this may seem too radical to some vendors, justifying it is not at all difficult: All information you need about how much and when and for what to pay your vendors is already in your databases. Invoices are redundant (wasteful) and can be eliminated. Here are the key data needed to do this:

- A part number
- Was it received?
- How many were received?
- Was a price established with the vendor?
- An address for the supplier
- The terms for the supplier

You may also need some new information to connect the daily shipment to the overall blanket agreement or purchase order to the supplier. The best way for IS to support this change is to become an active member of a cross-functional team, which also includes purchasing and accounting as well as most other departments in the company. It is almost impossible to implement kanban well without the full process stream of manufacturing, purchasing, engineering, accounting, and IS involvement. Implementing kanban across the company will be one of your longer and larger lean implementation objectives. The payback will be far greater than invoice elimination!

Other analytical system tools are also useful. Some worth considering and using actively follow:

- *Lowest material cost*: This customized program looks for the lowest available cost for all the parts in a BOM. The program or report displays the lowest costs compared with the actual cost for the built and shipped item. To help with the analysis, you display the vendor and order type of the lowest cost and actual cost. To manipulate this data, you export it to an Excel spreadsheet.

- *Shipped Cost*: In this macro report, the user enters the month required and the report shows the material cost as a percentage of gross sales price by the order, organized by product line. This provides an overview of the percentage of shipped order material throughout the month, grouped with similar products, and shows any material content errors prior to closing. This also positions you to detect and correct errors during the month rather than the end of the month when such activity will delay closing.

- *Error and exceptions*: It is appealing when planning a new system or enhanced system functionality, to plan for perfect execution of transactions. In the real world, no matter how diligent you are, errors, deviations, and the unexpected are, well, expected. If the deviation takes long to fix or requires special, extreme handling, then you clog the system and the data with confusing and wasteful transactions. Lean helps you approach errors and exceptions quickly and efficiently, mostly because the lean philosophy anticipates and thus accommodates potential glitches.

For example, think what would happen if an information system was not programmed to consider the possibility that a customer might pay more than was owed. In most ERP systems, there is no function to clear off an account excess, whether for large amounts or nickel-and-dime amounts. Over time this can clog accounts receivable with insignificant items, a wasteful nuisance. The lean solution is to build in cleanup protocols, to seek out the "normal" deviations, and to provide remedial tools.

Standard Allocations

With the use of Plain English Financials, the accounting team will probably want some special routines at month's end to allocate shared costs to multiple product, channel, or geographic slices of the business. These are different from allocations used in standard cost, as they are only at the macro-view level, not at the part level. Moreover, you will not aggregate these costs with the direct costs but show them explicitly as allocated costs. Usually, one of these views or slices will dominate (it is the product view in most lean companies). All are equally valuable, but you will need flexible methods to allocate them and one allocation tool will probably not be enough. For instance, in one department it might make sense to base allocation on a set percentage of the total cost each month. In another, it might make more sense to focus on a relationship to actual sales dollars or on a set dollar amount. The possibilities are endless, but flexibility is the key. Once established, you might not change the methods frequently. Usually, once you complete the allocation for a month, the amount booked in the allocation becomes static or historical for that month.

At the end of the day, flexibility and simple methods, used in a consistent format, are the critical factors that align your allocations to your lean organization's needs. A recent conceptual shift in lean thinking is that accounting is not the only source of information in the lean environment. Information that traditional companies kept in the general ledger, but were not really used from the ledger, will now be collected and used in the lean cell (on the shop floor or in the business process) or anywhere else people need it. One of the goals is to have lots of point data, collected manually or technologically, that will never be seen in the general ledger. In the end, such lean practices make accounting easier, less time-consuming, and less expensive.

As in traditional companies, the IS team and accounting will have a close relationship, but not because of complex standard cost data collection and reporting. They will work closely together to accommodate the new, flexible information needs of a lean company, with a focus on the future, not the past.

Seven Steps to Eliminating Standard Cost from an Information System

T HIS SIMPLE APPROACH is appropriate when a company's products are built in lean cellular manufacturing with few shared resources. The initial six accounting and system steps are listed below. Later, the accounting team will need to go through some analytical steps to value inventory at the end of the quarter or year.

1. *Create the departments.* These are the departments that will have the Income, Cost of Goods Sold, and Direct Expenses data for the Products. Each product line will have a financial statement that is consistent with the statement of the cellular manufacturing cell where the product is made.

2. *Add data to new departments.* Beginning in January (or the first month you select), point the invoiced revenue for the product to its department. Point the Cost of Goods Sold entries to the department. Put the salaries and related benefits, as well as other direct spending, in this department. The expenses will be only the direct expenses for that product. You will have the same account codes you have in other departments, but they will apply only to the products area.

In addition to changing the general ledger, the inventory and payroll systems will also need to point to these product departments. *If a person works some of the time in one product area and other times in another area, we recommend putting that person's cost in products for the days spent there. We usually do not fine-tune it closer than a day at a time.*

3. *Roll the cost in the Inventory system to change Labor and Overhead to zero.* Create a new account for the excess value eliminated from Inventory after the roll in the current asset section of the balance sheet. Create a name for this account; it might be Absorption Account, or Product Labor and Overhead Account (PLOA). The accountant will use this account only at the end of the quarter or year.

4. *Completion of a machine.* As a products' machine (or finished good) is completed and put into Inventory in January (or your first month of implementation), put ONLY the material content of that machine into inventory. This will be the only value in the inventory to post the cost roll. DO NOT ADD LABOR AND OVERHEAD TO INVENTORY. (See #6 below if you complete a machine that was in WIP on December 31st.)

5. *Shipping.* If you ship a machine that was put in inventory before January, expense ONLY the material component of that machine. Leave the Labor and Overhead value in inventory. This will stay here all year and be available for the accountant's end-of-year accrual.

6. *Conversion of WIP.* For the machines that were in WIP on December 31st, move the Labor and Overhead that was in inventory on December 31st to the PLOA. These machines will now be valued as the Material content only.

7. *Shipping new machines.* When you ship a machine that was added to in inventory in January, move only the Material values to Cost of Goods Sold. Beginning in January, Cost of Goods Sold will have only the Material for the products.

That is it! Basically, a machine goes in and out of inventory at Material. The Labor and Overhead (PLOA) you have in Inventory already stays there (from December 31st) and new Labor and Overhead is expensed as you incur it. At the end of the year, accounting will re-access the value of Labor and Overhead you have in WIP and Finished Goods and adjust the PLOA using a journal entry. For the IS team, there is little or no modification of core system capabilities; the team will use some of the features in new ways.

APPENDIX II

The Thirteen Guiding Information System Principles

1. Automate only if it is easier, faster, and complements your culture.
2. Build commonality to increase visibility and access to information.
3. The primary purpose of security is to avoid data corruption and provide information access.
4. Nothing lasts forever.
5. Systems and software inflexibility can be the greatest inhibitor of change.
6. Plain English-system instructions are better than shorthand.
7. Keystrokes matter to power users.
8. Capture everything you can about your customer.
9. Archive customer history; clean house on internal transactions.
10. Capture information once and be done.
11. Use commonality to create an information highway.
12. Productivity for all is more important than productivity for one.
13. Huge data stores are easy to manipulate.

INDEX

T

Y

ABOUT THE AUTHORS

Duane Jones has worn several hats at Lantech, and has served the company as material handler, engineering change coordinator, and production scheduler. When Lantech decided to go lean, he became a member of the kaizen team for the lean effort. After implementing Lantech's ERP system in 1995, he learned to program (without any previous experience) and subsequently trained others in the customization of the new ERP system. Duane then became Lantech's IS Team Leader, a position he holds to this day. In this capacity, he is responsible for hardware, software, and application integration in our company. He has served as consultant to Lantech's European affiliate during its ERP implementation in 2003 and continues to apply lean principles directly within IS as well as in any IS customer projects.

While at Lantech, Jean Cunningham was the company CFO and responsible for corporate services, HR, accounting, information systems, telecom, facilities, and many of the company's continuous improvement activities until 1999. Fluid in project responsibilities, she was appointed project sponsor for implementation of the ERP system in 1995 and was also involved with Lantech's very first manufacturing kaizen events in 1992, geared to implement lean on the factory shop floor. After leaving Lantech, Jean assumed a similar lean leader position while serving as CFO for a door manufacturing company that adopted lean as a business strategy. Jean frequently provides consulting services to companies interested in lean manufacturing, IS implementation in a lean environment, and lean accounting.